Mongolian Folktales

MONGOLIAN FOLKTALES

by
HILARY ROE METTERNICH

introduction by
DR. PUREVIIN KHORLOO

illustrated by
NOROVSAMBUUGIIN BAATARTSOG

PUBLISHED BY AVERY PRESS
IN ASSOCIATION WITH
THE UNIVERSITY OF WASHINGTON PRESS

*for Alexander,
who was not with us,
and for Matthias,
who was,
and for Cornel,
who makes everything possible*

© 1996 Avery Press, Inc.

published by Avery Press, Inc.
600 Kalmia Avenue, Boulder, CO 80304, USA
phone: 1-303-443-1592
email: kalmia6@aol.com

distributed by University of Washington Press
POBOX 50096, Seattle, WA 98145-5096, USA
phone: 1-800-441-4115
email: uwpord@u.washington.edu

Library of Congress Cataloguing-in-Publication Data
Mongolian Folktales/by Hilary Roe Metternich; introduction by Khorloo Pureviin; illustrated by Norovsambuugin Baatartsog.
      p.   cm.
    ISBN: 0-937321-06-0
    1. Tales–Mongolia. 2. Mongols–Folklore. I. Metternich, Hilary Roe. II. Pureviin, Khorloo. III. Baatartsog, Norovsambuugin.
GR337.5.M64   1996
398.2'0951'7–dc20   96-24687
                                            CIP

Table of Contents

Acknowledgments 11

Introduction by Dr. Pureviin Khorloo 13

About the illustrator, Norovsambuugiin Baatartsog 29

Folktales

How storytelling began among the Mongol People 33

How the Camel lost its Antlers and its Tail 37

The Clever Little Hedgehog 43

Did the Khan have a Head? 47

The Legend of Erkhii Mergen, the Archer 51

The Fox and the Lion 55

Why the Camel rolls in the Ashes 57

The Wise Judge 61

Why the Bat lives in the Dark 65

How a Small Rabbit saved a Large Horse 69

The Two Good Brothers 73

How the Chipmunk got its Stripes 77

The Four Friendly Animals 81

How the Wasp lost its Voice 85

The Flying Frog 89

FOLKTALES, *continued:*

    The Fox, the Wolf, and the Bag of Butter 93

    The Old Man and the Lion 97

    The Mouse who battled the Elephant 103

    The Turtle and the Monkey 107

    The Faithful Little Fox 111

    The Tale of the One-Eyed Frog and the Turtle 115

    The Fool and the Moon 119

    How the Hare split its Lip 121

    Why the Dog, Cat, and Mouse hate each other 125

    How Mangas the Monster met his End 129

Acknowledgments

The twenty-five stories presented here, classic examples of the folk tales of Mongolia, have come down to us via the oral tradition of the Mongolian nomadic peoples. This rich heritage has become accessible to most Westerners only recently: Mongolia began opening its doors to the outside world in 1990.

The stories in this collection were illustrated by the Mongol papercut artist, Norovsambuugiin Baatartsog. Each is cut freehand from a single piece of black paper.

Many of the stories were translated from the original Mongolian by Khorloogiin Bulgan. In editing them, I have made every effort to ensure that the content and spirit of the tales have remained essentially unchanged.

An introduction has been written by the distinguished scholar, Dr. Pureviin Khorloo. Now in his eighties, Dr. Khorloo was Chairman of the Institute of Language and Literature in the Mongolian Academy of Science for many years. He was personally involved in collecting and preserving the oral history of his country in a period when it was not easy to do so.

In acknowledging those who have contributed to this book, the people of Mongolia must come first. As Dr. Khorloo points out, even though Mongol traditions are changing, the wisdom of the old tales lives on.

Hilary Metternich

Introduction
by Dr. Pureviin Khorloo

ORIGINS OF MONGOLIAN FOLKTALES

It is hard to say when these folktales originated. We could, in fact, date the start of folktales to the time when people first started talking to each other. This is true all over the world, not just in Mongolia. Tarvaa, for instance, is just a name. Nobody knows if there ever was such a man, or whether he died in such and such a plague. There were so many plagues on our land, and the story tells only about one among many. But then again nobody can confirm that there wasn't such a man.

Is the story about Blind Tarvaa really how storytelling began in Mongolia? This is not strictly a folktale but what we call a legend, a *domog.* Legends have some evidence to support them, some basis in reality, whereas stories, which we call *tuul,* are merely stories.

Blind Tarvaa tells about a man who is poor. One of our Mongolian proverbs says that someone who is poor is often a dreamer. He dreams, he invents tales, and what he dreams he tells in stories. Tarvaa is blind. He is disabled and therefore challenged. An orphan easily becomes a storyteller: storytelling is connected with emotions, the spirit, a vision of the world. The image of Tarvaa is the image of a man who represents common people. The story of Tarvaa means, in a sense, the profound and simple fact that stories are generated and passed along by normal people.

Folklore is the most ancient part of the Mongolian cultural heritage. It was created long before our various scripts were invented. Is the Blind Tarvaa story about the beginning of storytelling in Mongolia true? People give birth to their heritage and their tales: that is true and as ancient as humans.

VARIATION AMONG FOLKTALES

Mongolian folktales come in as many variations as there are storytellers. Ours is not a rigid tradition. Take, for example, the story that talks about a camel, an animal who most unfortunately lost his horns and his tail.

The story about the camel is a myth. We define myths as fairy tales based on legends. The story about the camel who lost his antlers is told here in the form of a fairy tale. All stories about animals actually represent people, they are people. The horse and the deer in this story represent very cunning people, people who lie in order to gain profit. Though the characters are given the qualities of animals, human beings identify with them and recognize themselves in these creatures. The camel, of course, represents virtue. He is fair. He believes what people say, he helps others without hesitation. The deer usually represents a negative image in our folktales. A deer does not keep his promises.

Now to return to the question of variation among tales. The horse is rather negative in this story. But this is only one version of the story, one variant. In central Mongolia the horse figure would be represented by a tiger, a *bar*. The tricky horse would be more common in the far west of Mongolia. This is a typical form of the freedom of variation, which again proves that each storyteller recreates his own version of the world.

TYPES OF FOLKTALES

Mongolian folktales have been classified by those who have studied them into the following five general groups: those about animals, those about magic and especially the magical horse, those about domestic affairs, satirical tales, and, lastly, tales about relations between man and nature or about the origins of nature. This last category is believed to be the most ancient.

The story about the Khan's head is an example that belongs to the domestic affairs category. This genre tells tales about ordinary people and the social relations and conflicts that go on among them. Since these tales reflect everyday life, they are the most numerous and are frequently enriched with endless variations. In the story of the Khan's head, even the wife of the Khan was terrified of him. He was so tyrannical and cruel that she never looked him straight in the eye. This story also reflects the tension between those who have power and those who lack power.

One of the most beloved categories of folktales is magical folktales. This genre often uses a hero, a "ragged fellow," named Nusgai Jur. The horse of this ragged fellow possesses magical strength and can cover distances of years in months and distances of months in hours. He has wings, like the wings you see on many of the magical horses in this book. Nusgai Jur helps people in distress and is generally known to bring happiness and peace.

Satirical tales are perhaps the most political of the various genres. These stories are often told in the voice of the travelling lama, Badarchin. They are used to poke fun at and demean people who would like to gain some measure of control over you. They are like verbal weapons.

Many of the stories selected for this book relate to animals—these stories tend to exhibit a humorous approach. To Mongolians, different animals represent different human attributes. The hedgehog, for example, is not regarded as a good animal. If a hedgehog comes into your home it is very bad luck. People are quite superstitious about this. Hedgehogs usually conceal their faces—they walk along with their heads down, and so are not regarded by Mongolians as creatures that are open and frank. In the hedgehog story in this book, however, the animal is used to make a contrast with the wolf and fox. To my way of thinking, the hedgehog in this story doesn't represent someone who is clever, but rather someone who is cunning, even more cunning than a fox or a wolf.

Mongolians often use the bristly backs of hedgehogs to ward off bad spirits. A spiny hedgehog skin placed over a doorway is a good guardian against bad things coming into the house. This applies in particular to snakes, since it is not uncommon for snakes to slip into Mongolian *gers*. Hedgehogs eat snakes in real life. People put the skinned backs of hedgehogs up above a door to make sure no snakes or snake-spirits come in. The snake, mind you, has an even worse image than a hedgehog in Mongolia.

The story about the fox and the lion runs along the same general lines as the one about the hedgehog. Now there are no lions in Mongolia, of course, but at one time there may have been, when the temperature was warmer. There are many Mongolian geographic place-names that include the word lion, *arslan* in Mongolian. For example, Arslan Uul, Lion Mountain, to name one. The lion is one of the Four Strong Animals in Mongolian lore. The four are: Lion, Dragon, Elephant, and Garuda. The symbol of Ulaanbaatar is a garuda, a mythical animal that came into Mongolia from India via Tibet. The garuda is the guardian deity of Bogd Uul, the mountain south of Ulaanbaatar. There are many folktales about all of these Strong Animals.

POETRY, MUSIC, EPICS, AND FOLKTALES

Music, poetry, epics, folktales and regular speech do not have the same clear dividing lines in Mongolia that they perhaps have elsewhere. The verbal arts were among our earliest arts and have been paramount in this country of nomads.

In the Mongolian culture, great stress has been placed upon personal skills, in particular intellectual skills, oratorical skills, and all kinds of verbal and vocal arts. As a nomadic people moving from place to place on the steppe, it was necessary that baggage be as light as possible. One's main assets included a finely honed ability to express oneself. The Mongolian language is well suited to the position it has played in the transmission of Mongolian culture. It is a Ural-Altaic language, but its vocabulary includes a rich amalgamation of

many languages: the word for book, one example among many, is derived from the Greek. In addition, the language is rich in the subtleties of description that are the natural consequence of very close observation of nature.

As a result, the verbal arts in Mongolia have included a great appreciation for rhythm, alliteration, all the aurally pleasing devices that can be used to communicate the range of human emotions. In Mongolia, songs, poetry, and folktales were not related to the written word until much later in their development than in agrarian societies. Folktales, proverbs, and songs had a tremendous importance in daily life.

It is difficult at times to obtain paper today in Ulaanbaatar. One can imagine how difficult it was before. Things were not generally written down. They were committed to memory and transmitted through the medium of the voice. The voice could either sing or speak, and was often, although not always, accompanied by music.

Mongolian music has been divided into *tuul,* an essentially narrative form, and long-song, *urtiin duu,* and short-song, *bogino duu,* essentially singing. The word *tuul* means epic: it relates stories about a hero. Texts of *tuul* were comprised of many units of generally four lines each. The longest known epic has a total of 20,000 lines. The person narrating a *tuul* had to have high mental concentration as well as a talent for communication.

The oldest examples of *tuul* date from the thirteenth century. Folktales are not, generally speaking, classified as *tuul,* but many of the same qualities apply to both. They stem from the same everyday lives of herdsmen and reflect the hopes and the wry wisdom of a hardy people.

The horse is often the hero of all these oral forms, and of Mongolian life in general. In this book, you will notice many images of flying horses, as well as several depictions of the instrument called the *moriin huur,* horsehead fiddle.

The Mongolian language has a number of different words for horse. The term that is used for the instrument is *mori,* not a mare and not a stallion but the horse that has been gelded and is used every day for riding. Horses are immensely important in Mongolia, for food and drink, especially *airak,* and for transport. The word for fortunate in Mongolian is *morisaitai,* someone who owns a good horse. Healthy in Mongolian is *xiimori,* flying horse, or celestial horse. The relationship of trust between man and horse lies at the heart of many folktales and songs. As for the word *huur,* it means lute. It is not known when the *huur* began to be used in Mongolia—there are many theories and many folktales regarding this question, but it should be understood that the *morin huur* is only one of several bowed instruments in Mongolia, and that different regions of Mongolia use different kinds of *moriin huur.* The first historically known *huurch,* or player of *huur,* was Argasan who lived in the thirteenth century.

MONGOLIAN CULTURE AS RETAINED IN MONGOLIAN FOLKTALES

Mongolians have used ten distinct scripts that can be identified in the centuries of their written history. The origin of these scripts relates to Hunnu markings, Turkic runes, then later Uighur and other scripts, but the written tradition was built upon the foundation of a very strong oral tradition. What came to be written down, such as the Geser or other classics, had formed a part of the historical memory of our people for a very long time.

This oral tradition incorporated many elements of the most ancient Mongolian culture. Particularly since historical memory has become muted in the changes of the past century, folktales are important bearers of our past. From folktales we can dimly make out some of our original beliefs, as well as identify how certain elements entered the Mongolian tradition from other lands. The story of the Ramayana, for example, is known to have entered Mongolia

by at least the fourteenth century, when it started exerting a strong influence on the development of Mongolian heroic epics.

Or take the story in this book about the camel who is denied the privilege of being written into the cycle of twelve animals. The camel is considered to be a very fine animal: reserved, kind, generous, and very trusting of others. Though he looks so huge, there is a contrast between his character and his appearance; the tiny mouse turns out to be more cunning and so gets himself included in the zodiac.

When did this way of describing a calendar begin in Mongolia? The sixty-year cycle, including the animals of the zodiac, is believed to have been introduced into Mongolia during the reign of the Khitans. Khitan coins minted in the tenth to twelfth centuries are stamped on the back with a picture of the animal of the year in which the coin was made. Chinggis Khan had golden coins minted in 1209 that have all twelve animals on the reverse side. Dates in the Secret History of the Mongols are given in terms of this animal cycle. For example, we see passages such as, "In the autumn of the year of the dog [1226], Chinggis Khan set forth against the Tangut people." The Secret History was written in Mongolian in around the year 1240. The animals in Mongolia are the same as those used in China, Japan, Korea and elsewhere in Asia. Although we call ours the Mongolian calendar, this is an oriental tradition, not just Mongolian.

Going to more ancient history, take the story of Erkhii Mergen, narrated in this book. This tale dates from at least the twelfth century, but is in all likelihood much earlier. It tells a myth about how the world was created, indeed how people became people. Erkhii Mergen turns into a marmot in the end, and this interpretation of marmots goes back to very ancient times. The tale of Erkhii Mergen and similar stories comes from the time when people first started to learn about nature and to question how nature was created. Such myths usually speculate about the beginnings of things, animals, and people.

Do people really believe the Erkhii Mergen myth? Since it is a myth you can believe it or not, as you wish. But it is most likely that many Mongolian people do believe the story. It is very deeply rooted in our culture. As evidence of this, for example, to this day people do not eat the small piece of meat in the animal that is called *hun makh,* or man meat. This piece, near the liver, is usually cut off and thrown away. There is no scientific reason for not eating it—people could eat it, but they don't.

In general, whatever the type of tale and whatever its message, you will find that it relates essential characteristics of Mongolian people. These are: a sense of humor, a dignified etiquette, a deeply-rooted feeling of social relations and the social order, a feeling for ethical and aesthetic values, and a spiritual eye that has an acute appreciation of the powers of Nature.

THE STORYTELLER

Anybody could be a storyteller, not just an elder. Traditionally, though, it was older people who carried on the tradition. We have a saying that there are as many variations of a folktale as the number of people who tell it. This again is unlike our written literature.

All different kinds of storytellers narrated heroic epics, folktales, and another genre known as *bensen ulger,* renditions of Mongolian translations of Chinese literature. Heroic epics, especially in western Mongolia, were nearly always recited to the accompaniment of the *huur* or other instruments. In central Mongolia and eastern Mongolia, such epics were generally recited unaccompanied. In contrast, *bensen ulger* were always recited to *huur* in the area including central Mongolia and what is now Inner Mongolia.

Each region, therefore, had variations not just of content, but of style of recitation, type of instrument, and narrator. In some areas old men generally sang or recited, in some areas women sang. The telling of tales and epics was not confined to one class of person or

one chosen elder. Anyone could and did tell stories, because the telling, and the singing, was an active part of Mongolian daily life.

COLLECTING THE TALES

Nowadays it is difficult to find the same kind of living oral tradition. It was still flourishing, however, in the early part of this century. The Institute of Mongolian Language and Literature of the Academy of Sciences was founded in Ulaanbaatar in 1921. From that time, Mongolian people themselves started thinking more about their own cultural heritage. In the 1920s and 1930s there were still people in the country telling stories. Eventually few remained, and now there are essentially none. Young people in our country now know very little about the tradition. Some of it is still remembered by older people in their seventies and eighties. At eighty years old, I am one of them.

I collected a number of stories in my early days, while assembling material for my PhD dissertation on Mongolian oral traditions. For example, in 1957 I went to Bulgan *sum* in Hovd *aimag,* in the northwest of the country. There I met a man, an old man, then sixty-three years old, whose name was Buyan. He was of the Urianhai nationality and was famous for his epics. He knew seven whole epics and could recite them verse by verse. I spent weeks living with him in his *ger,* writing down just two of the seven epics, the Zul Aldar Khan and Uyan Mongun Hadaasun. These two epics are really the same story: the first concerns the father and the second the son. I would spend nights in his *ger,* sitting and listening and writing.

There are many epics in Mongolia, not just these two or these seven. And there are many folktales, many more than the few in this book. It was clear that most of these were being lost, through the changes that began to occur in Mongolia in the twentieth century. I was Chairman of the Institute of Language and Literature in the Academy of Sciences for many years, so I sent a group of research fellows and scholars throughout Mongolia to collect what we could of these stories on tape. Back when I visited Buyan in Hovd aimag, we unfortunately had no tape recorders—so when I was doing this I wrote the whole epic down by hand in old Mongolian script.

NATURE OF THE ORAL TRADITION

In the archives of the Institute there are now a number of taped stories told by storytellers, as well as oral folktales that have been written down. Scholars sit in the library and listen to these tapes. They don't go around the countryside to collect tales. First, there are no old storytellers left. Second, what it was possible to find has mostly already been collected. Scholars study the material at a desk. I must say this is very different from hearing a live voice reciting a tale. The storytellers were noble people, whose memory held many things. They seemed to have a special aura around them. More than just the words, the way they told a story was inspiring.

One form of oral tradition still carries on, however. Mongolians want very much to preserve their cultural heritage. From a young age, children are told stories by their parents: although the stories have often acquired a modern cast, the wisdom and the spirit of the old folktales is continuing. Textbooks of secondary school students in Mongolia now include what are recognized as important elements of Mongolian culture: folktales, proverbs, parts of epics, riddles, fairytales, myths and legends. For students of linguistics in the University, it is mandatory to take a course in Mongolian folktales.

I consider Mongolian folktales to be a part of the cultural heritage of the world. Thanks to the efforts of Hilary Metternich and the vivid papercuts of Mr. Baatartsog this book will open a window onto Mongolian tales for a broader readership. As a scholar of Mongolian folklore, I would like to express my deep appreciation to Hilary Metternich for her valuable contribution in expanding the borders of these Mongolian tales and her active interest in the cultural tradition of the Mongol peoples.

About the Illustrator

Norovsambuugiin Baatartsog was the inspiration behind this book. Baatartsog introduced himself to me, the American wife of the German Ambassador to the Republic of Mongolia, at our Embassy in the capital of Ulaanbaatar where my husband and I were posted from February 1994 to 1996. The artist was hoping to sell some of his "silhouettes" or paper cuts to augment his teaching income.

I was so impressed by Baatartsog's work that I purchased his cards, commissioned more, and began wondering about the possibility of collaborating on a project to make his work and the art of the Mongol paper cut known to a wider audience. The idea of a collection of classic Mongol folktales illustrated by a Mongol artist in a traditional Mongol medium was conceived.

Although silhouette cutting dates only to around 1950, the Mongolians have nevertheless had a long tradition of cutting shapes out of a variety of other materials. Small animals are cut out of thick felt to decorate carpets and as children's toys; geometric shapes are cut out of different colored leather and silver to embellish saddles or boots. The Mongolian appliquéed religious *thankas*, with hundreds of pieces of cut and layered cloth, are famous throughout Buddhist countries for their intricacy and refinement.

While creative paper cutting in general can be viewed as an extension of this long and well-developed Mongol tradition, Norovsambuugiin Baatartsog has carried the art to an unusual degree of sophistication. He is a master of the Mongolian paper cut. His complex scenes, based mostly on Mongol themes, require unusual dexterity and powers of concentration. Fine points of light, details of fur and sunbeams, and facial expressions of both humans and animals are achieved with nothing more than scissors and paper. The artist explains that once an idea is in his head, his imagination begins working. He stares for a few moments at a single, blank piece of black paper and the layout of the picture emerges by itself. He begins to liberate it, freehand, from the paper with his four-inch pair of scissors.

Norovsambuugiin Baatartsog was born in 1965 in Khovd *aimag,* the westernmost of the twenty-one Mongol provinces. Khovd is nestled in the shadows of the snowy Altai mountain range. He studied in Ulaanbaatar at the Pedagogical University of Mongolia in the Faculty of Fine Arts and Design, graduating as a professional book illustrator and teacher in 1990. His thesis addressed the art of the Mongol papercut.

Between 1989 and 1991, Baatartsog had three one-man shows of his work in Ulaanbaatar where his graphics, papercuts, and Mongolian "flat" paintings, similar to primitive painting, were exhibited. His reputation as one of Mongolia's most talented young artists continues to grow.

Baatartsog is deeply committed to perpetuating the culture of Mongolia. To this end, he has created an art program for children that he hopes "will draw them to the customs and culture of their country so that the traditional heritage of the Mongolian peoples may endure." This effort should be especially applauded as Mongolia becomes increasingly exposed to and influenced by the West.

Baatartsog lives in Ulaanbaatar with his wife and two children, and teaches at the Institute of Design. This is the first time the artist has put his imagination and small, sharp scissors to work in illustrating a collection of Mongolian stories.

Hilary Metternich

self-portrait of the artist, who is left-handed

How Storytelling Began Among the Mongol People

A long, long time ago, the terrible Black Plague descended on Central Asia and began its assault on the people of Mongolia. Thousands, young and old, died a quick but painful death; those caught in the plague's deadly clutches had no chance of surviving. Men and women who remained healthy tried to save their lives. Fleeing in panic, they cried out to each other:

"We must try to escape! Fate will decide the Destiny of the suffering!"

Among the sick was a ten-year-old boy called Tarvaa. For days Tarvaa's body battled the forces of Death, but finally, weak and feverish, the young man lost all awareness of this world.

Tarvaa's spirit thought that young Tarvaa had died. It rose up out of the boy's body and began the sad journey to the Underworld. After many difficulties, the spirit of Tarvaa arrived before the portal of the Kingdom of the Underworld and was led to the presence of its Great Khan.

The Khan was most surprised to see such a young spirit. He asked sternly, "Why did you leave your body while it was still alive? Why are you here in my Kingdom?"

Trembling with fright, the spirit replied, "Begging your pardon, Great Khan, but all my family and all my friends who remained in that World stood over my body and said I was dead. Then they ran away. I did not wait for the terrible last moment, but simply left on my journey to you."

The Khan was touched by the simplicity and honesty of Tarvaa's spirit. He told the spirit gently, "Young spirit, your Time has not yet come. You do not belong here. You must return to your master. But before you set out on your long journey home, I will grant you one gift. You may choose and take back with you anything from my Kingdom that you desire."

It was only then that the spirit of Tarvaa looked about him. As far as his eye could see in the dim light of the Kingdom of the Underworld were every Pleasure and every Pain to be had in Life: Wealth and Poverty, Good Fortune and Bad, Happiness and Sadness, Music and Song, Rich Food and Clothing, Amusement and Laughter, Ballads and Dance, and many, many other temptations, both good and bad.

The spirit of Tarvaa wandered among all these wondrous treasures for some time. It looked to the right, then to the left, but selected nothing. Only after a long search did it finally stop and stare: it had spied the one thing that Tarvaa was to value most in life.

Hesitatingly, the spirit pointed to something deep in the shadows, then looked back questioningly in the direction of the Khan. The Great Khan nodded his consent with a fatherly smile.

This is how the gift of Tales and Legends was bestowed upon the spirit of Tarvaa.

The Khan then instructed the spirit, "Now return home at once. Use this gift well in Life, and do not come here again until you have been called!"

After days and nights, the spirit finally reached the body of Tarvaa. To its distress, it found that a crow had dug out Tarvaa's eyes in its absence. Though sad and frightened by the terrible condition of its now sightless body, the spirit did not dare disobey the orders of the Khan. Silently, it slipped back into the boy's still-sleeping flesh.

Young Tarvaa recovered from the fearsome Black Plague and, though blind, lived to be an old, old man. Throughout his long life, Tarvaa would travel to the far corners of the Mongol lands recounting wonderful Tales and Legends to his people. They were stories not only from his own country, but also delightful tales that he learned from faraway lands.

In this way, Blind Tarvaa, known and loved by Mongolians as the greatest storyteller of all time, used well the gift bestowed upon his spirit by the Great Khan of the Kingdom of the Underworld.

How the Camel Lost its Antlers and its Tail

Many years ago, when the Camel had magnificent, twelve-branched antlers and a long, luxurious tail, the Deer was an ugly-looking, bald-headed beast. And the Horse, well, the poor Horse had almost no tail at all with which to shoo away the flies. This, as you can imagine, tended to make him irritable.

Although the Camel was pleased to have such splendid refinements adorning his clumsy body, he didn't take any special care of them or even think about them very much. He was, to be truthful, completely unaware that his antlers and his tail could cause jealousy in the other animals, that other animals might try all kinds of tricks so that they could have his unique gifts as their own. Perhaps he should have paid more attention because, one day, this is what happened in the life of the Camel.

At noon on a hot summer's day, the Camel, especially thirsty, strolled down to the lake for a long, refreshing drink. When he had quenched his thirst, he raised his head and paused for some moments, gazing across the deep blue water at the distant mountains, swishing his long, full tail this way and that. Because of his great height and all of his protrusions and accoutrements, the Camel looked quite splendid as he stood there in the sun.

From the forest surrounding the lake, a bald-headed Deer emerged. Sighting the Camel and admiring his impressive horns, the Deer's eyes narrowed slyly. When he neared the Camel, the Deer stopped and bowed, his face now masked with sadness. Sighing, he said,

"Good afternoon, Mr. Camel. How are you today?"

The Camel, thinking, 'My Heavens! Isn't the Deer a funny-looking fellow!' grinned his toothy grin and cheerily replied:

"Why, thankyou, Mr. Deer. I couldn't be better. But you? Whatever is the matter? You seem so sad."

"Yes," sighed the Deer. "I am sad. Very sad. Tonight I'm invited to a celebration. All the forest animals from far and wide will be there with their fancy furs and flashy plummage. Oh, how can I possibly go there with this hideous, bald head? I'm so ugly and plain!"

Then, tears starting in his eyes, the Deer cried:

"Oh, Mr. Camel! I dream every night about having wonderful antlers like yours! Would it be possible? Could you? Oh, dear Mr. Camel! Please let me borrow your antlers—just for tonight! I beg you!"

You can imagine how surprised the Camel was by the Deer's sudden and unexpected request. Part with his antlers? Why, he'd never done such a thing! But the Deer looked so forlorn and was now, in fact, beginning to sob with self-pity.

So the Camel, from his great height, with half-closed eyes, looked down on the unattracive Deer and said:

"Well, Mr. Deer, all right. I will agree to let you use my antlers, but only for tonight. You must return them to me at daylight."

"I promise," swore the Deer. "I promise you, noble Mr. Camel, that I will return your antlers first thing tomorrow morning when you come to the lake for a drink!"

So saying, the Deer fixed the magnificent branches to his bald head and hurried back into the forest. For the first time in his life he felt handsome and powerful. He strutted along the forest paths with head held high. Soon the Deer met up with Mr. Horse.

"Well, hello, Mr. Deer!" said the astonished Horse, marvelling at his suddenly royal-looking friend. "And where did you get those splendid antlers?"

The Deer recounted his story, which gave Mr. Horse his own idea. Bidding Mr. Deer farewell, he hastened down to the lake hoping that Mr. Camel had not headed home. To his relief, there was the Camel munching on the tall green grass. The Horse called out:

"Good afternoon, Mr. Camel! And how are you this hot day?"

After some small pleasantries during which the Horse tried not to laugh

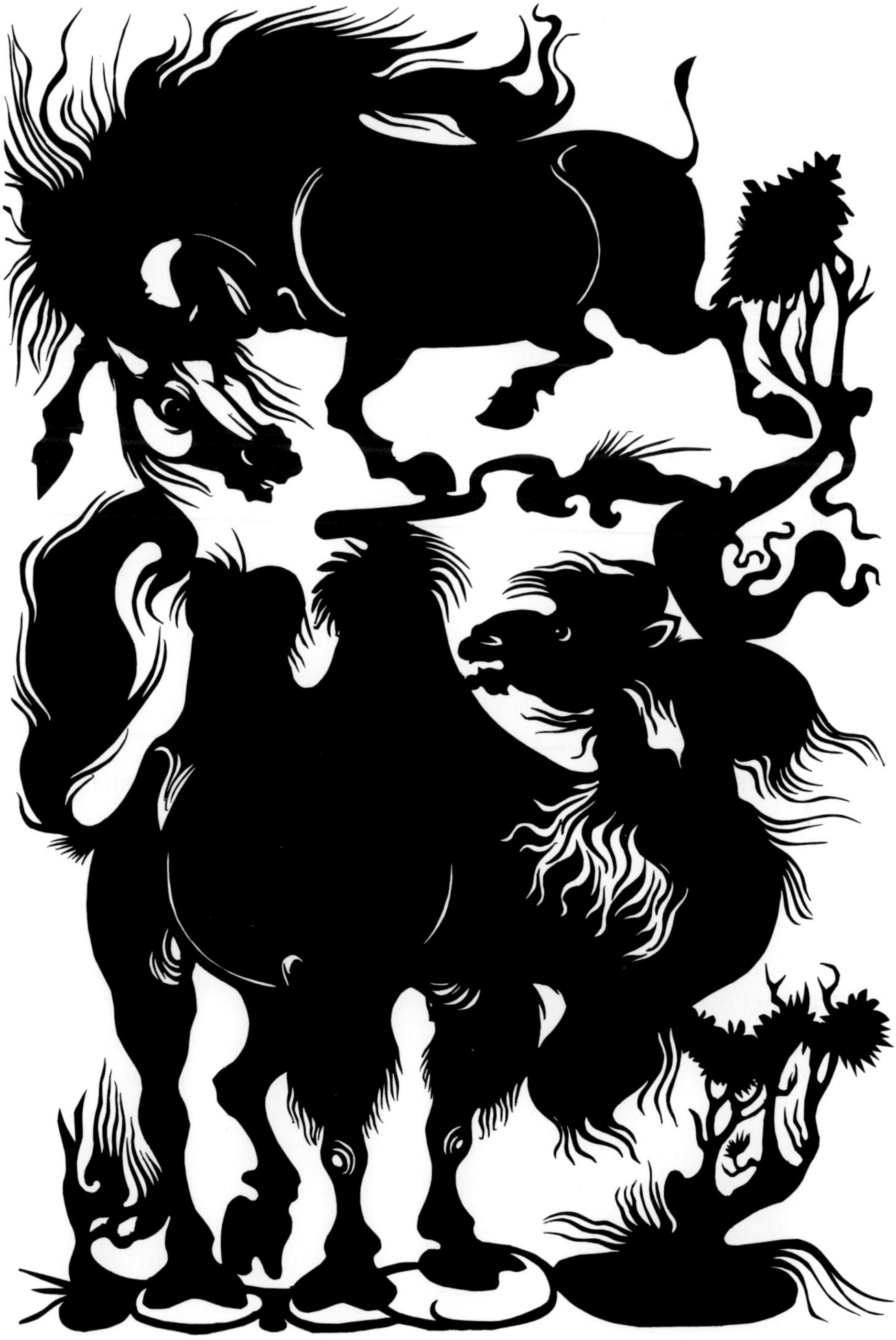

out loud at the now bald-headed Camel, he asked to borrow the Camel's luxurious tail for the forest celebration, explaining,

"I would be eternally grateful, kind Mr. Camel, as it would improve my appearance enormously!"

Considering that since he'd already lent out his antlers, it probably wouldn't hurt to lend out his tail as well for only one night, the Camel agreed. He admonished the Horse:

"But you must return it to me at daybreak!"

Securely attaching the long hair to his rump, the horse gave his word:

"I promise. I promise you, generous Mr. Camel, that I will return your tail first thing tomorrow morning when you come to the lake for a drink!"

And off the Horse trotted into the forest, swishing and swoshing that long, full tail, the most delighted horsey smile you can imagine spread across his big horsey face.

I think you know what happened. The Deer and the Horse, so mesmerized by the beauty (and practicality) of their splendid new features, did not come to the lake the next day. Nor did they come the next week or the next month. The Deer and the Horse, in fact, never came to the Camel at all to return his magnificent antlers and his luxurious tail.

Each time the Camel spied one of the two rascals, he would call out, begging them to be true to their word. The Horse would just neigh with laughter and gallop away; while the Deer would sneer scornfully and tell the Camel:

"I'll return your antlers when the billy-goat's horns grow up to the heavens, and when the foolish Camel's stubby tail grows down to the earth!"

Which, of course, meant: Never.

And so, from that day till now, whenever the Camel drinks from a pool of water and sees his bare head reflected, he shakes it with disbelief and sadness. After only a few sips, he raises his long neck and gazes hard across the steppe, looking carefully from one mountain to another. The trusting Camel still believes that the Deer will appear on the horizon or that the Horse will come galloping towards him with apologies.

You might like to know that the Deer and the Horse have not gone unpunished for their deceit. Oh, no. The Horse was tamed by Man, who then clipped his tail, clamped a heavy saddle on his back, and put him to work.

No longer does the Horse spend his whole life freely roaming the wide Mongolian steppe, swishing the Camel's thick tail this way and that.

As proof that they do not belong to him, the antlers of the Deer, once every year, fall right off his head. While the Deer waits for a new pair, he has to sneak around the forest with his ugly old bald head exposed for all the world to see. The animals, all of whom know this tale, laugh and point a knowing finger, while the Deer quickly runs away in shame.

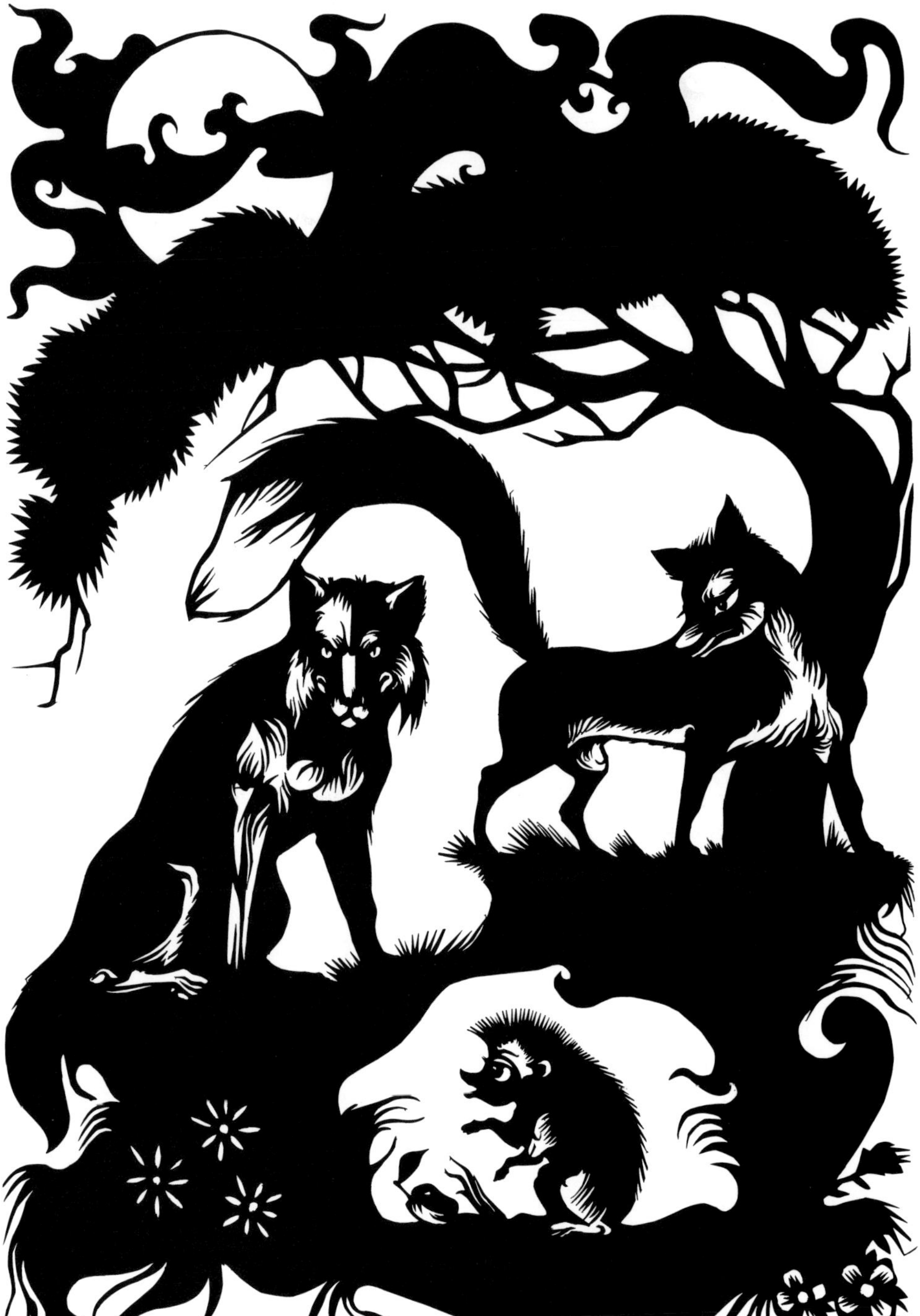

THE CLEVER LITTLE HEDGEHOG

Once upon a time, a Wolf, a Fox, and a Hedgehog lived together on the rolling steppes of Mongolia. One day, a long caravan of camels bearing all manner of goods from faraway lands passed near their home. When the dust raised by the caravan had settled, the three friends discovered a little plum that had fallen from one of the many sacks.

The animals had heard about plums, but none had ever seen one, let alone tasted one. They began to discuss which of them should have the privilege of eating this exoic fruit: there was only enough for one.

After a long debate, the friends finally agreed to a contest. It was the Wolf who had the idea:

"I know!" he cried. "I think the one who gets drunk on *airak** the quickest should have the pleasure of eating this plum!"

Thinking, of course, that he would win, the Wolf continued:

"As for me, I get drunk after just one sip of *airak!*"

The Fox was next to speak, and knowing that he was much smarter than the Wolf, he said: "That's nothing! I get drunk just by smelling *airak!*"

The last to speak was the Hedgehog, whom the others looked down upon because he was so small. He told his friends:

"Well, it's very sad for me, but I get drunk just hearing about *airak!*"

And with that, the Hedgehog swayed as if he were drunk.

The other animals had to admit that this clearly made the Hedgehog the winner. But before the Hedgehog could open his mouth to eat his prize, the envious Fox shouted:

"Wait! I have another idea. We need a second contest. I think that the one of us who runs the fastest should get to eat the plum!"

They all agreed to this second match, and prepared themselves for the race. The Hedgehog, who knew he stood no chance of winning because of his short legs, had already thought of a trick.

As the Wolf and the Fox took off in a cloud of dust, the Hedgehog caught hold of the fluffy tail of the Fox, and held on tight.

Just before the speedy Fox crossed the finish line, he stopped and looked back to check where the others were. At that moment, the little Hedgehog dropped off his tail, scurried under his belly, and from the winning side of the finish line called out:

"Well, hello there Mr. Fox! Hello Mr. Wolf! I see you've finally arrived! What took you so long?"

This is how the Hedgehog also won the second contest.

As the Wolf and the Fox looked on enviously, the clever little Hedgehog gobbled up the plum.

And a plum never tasted better.

*Airak: a Mongolian drink made from fermented mare's milk.

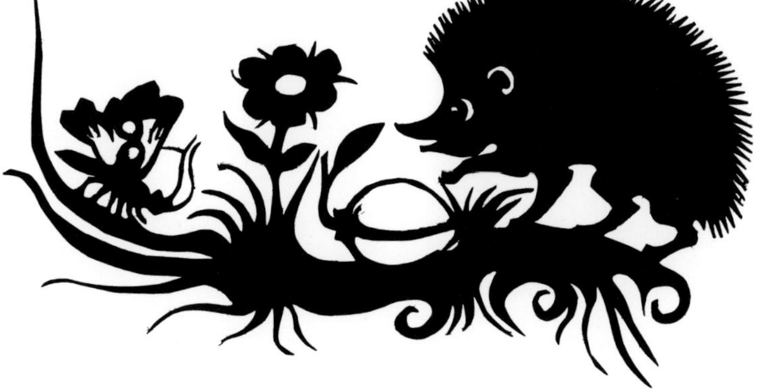

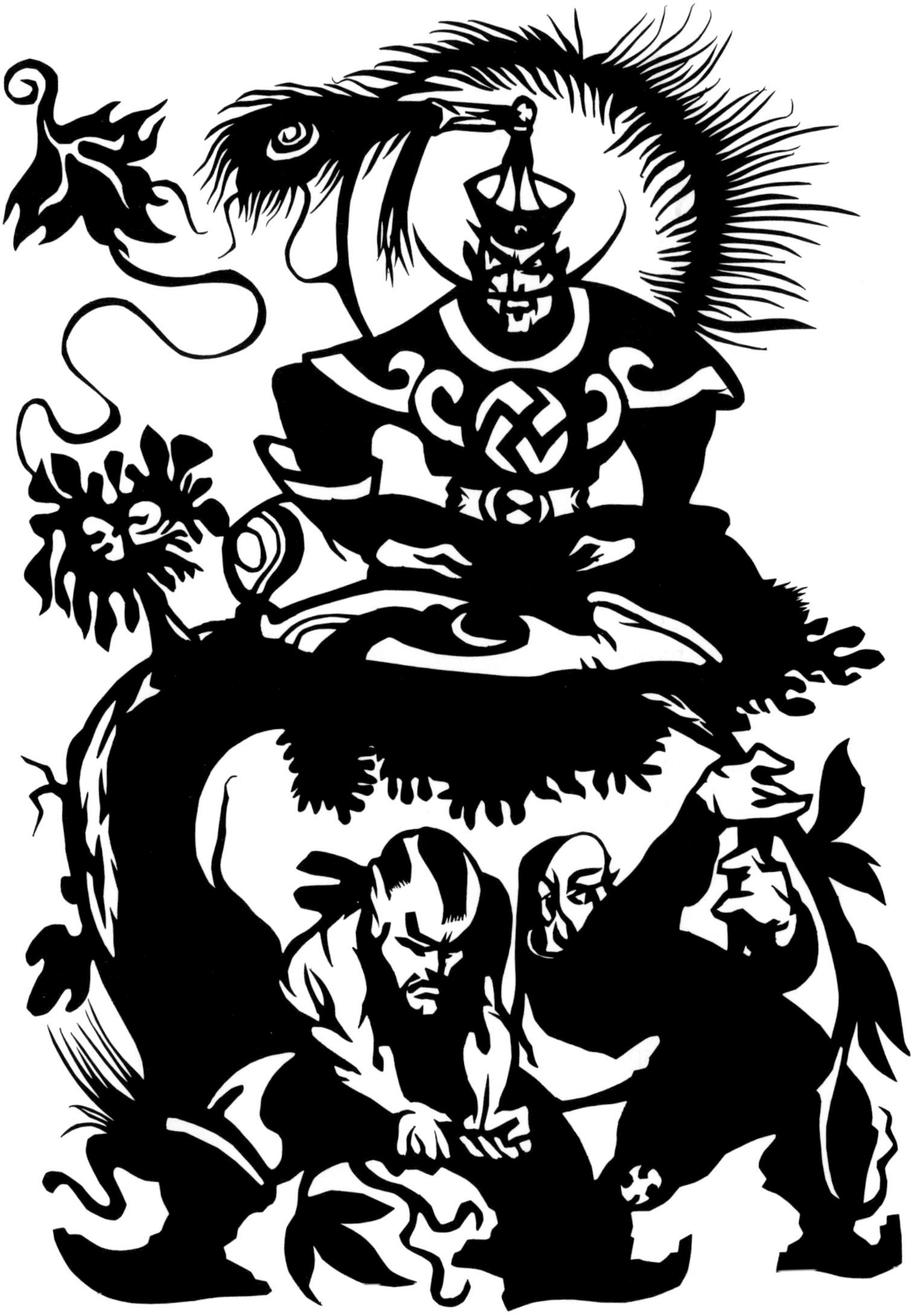

DID THE KHAN HAVE A HEAD?

Long, long ago there lived a wicked Mongol Khan who ruled harshly and was greatly feared by all his many subjects. The people were, in fact, so afraid of the Khan that no one had the courage to look him in the face.

One morning, the Khan, surrounded by his noblemen and followed by his many servants, decided to go hunting on the steppe.

After a long, hard day, feeling tired, he commanded his entourage to stop for a rest near a solitary tree. The Khan did not wish to sit on the ground with all the other noblemen, even though his servants had brought thick carpets and silk pillows to make him comfortable.

"I am the Khan!" he exclaimed. "I should sit above you all!"

Turning to his servants, he ordered:

"Bend this tree over to make me a seat so that I can enthrone myself like the Buddha on his lotus!"

The servants quickly obeyed their Master and with enormous effort bent down the branches of the strong tree. The Khan climbed up, but as he seated himself on his leafy throne, the ropes groaned and suddenly gave way. With great force, the tree sprang upright, flinging the Khan high in the air. Hitting the ground with a horrible thud, the Khan's body lay motionless. The great Khan was dead!

When the horrified noblemen and servants ran to their Master, they gasped. The body of the Khan had no head! How could this be? Either the Khan's head had been torn off by the force of the springing bough...or...the Khan never had a head!

Servants and noblemen stood together muttering and scratching their brows, bewildered. They asked:

"Do you recall if the Khan had a head on his shoulders? Do you?"

But no one seemed to know. No one could remember.

When you think about it, this was not surprising because all the people, men and women alike, had been afraid to raise their eyes in his presence.

At last an old servant spoke:

"I know what we should do. Let's go to the Khan's Counsellor. He conferred with the Khan every single day. Surely he should know whether the Khan had a head."

They all agreed that this was an excellent idea and galloped off on their horses to consult the Khan's Counsellor.

"This is how it happened," they explained. "We servants were trying to carry out the Khan's orders to enthrone him on the tree, but the Khan was thrown into the air and died. When we ran to him we saw that he had no head. Where could his head be? Did you, oh Counsellor, ever see a head on the shoulders of the Khan?"

"I don't know, brothers," said the Counsellor shaking his grey locks. "I was afraid to look at the Khan's face myself. I only know that he had a velvet hat with the Khan's round red ruby on the top."

"What do you advise us to do now?" asked the noblemen and servants.

"Perhaps you should go to the Khan's wife," replied the Counsellor. "Surely she ought to know whether or not her husband had a head."

The baffled men rushed off to the Khan's wife and told her the whole story. At the end they asked:

"Your majesty, could you answer just one simple question for us? Did the Khan have a head on his shoulders?"

Lowering her eyes in embarrassment, the Khan's wife said haltingly:

"Well...to tell you the truth, I really don't know. I know he had a moustache because it prickled when he kissed me. But you see, being afraid of the Khan, I screwed up my eyes so I never saw his face. I'm sorry I can't help you. I do not know if the Khan had a head."

And no matter who the noblemen and the servants asked, no one could remember if the Khan actually did have a head on his shoulders.

What do you think?

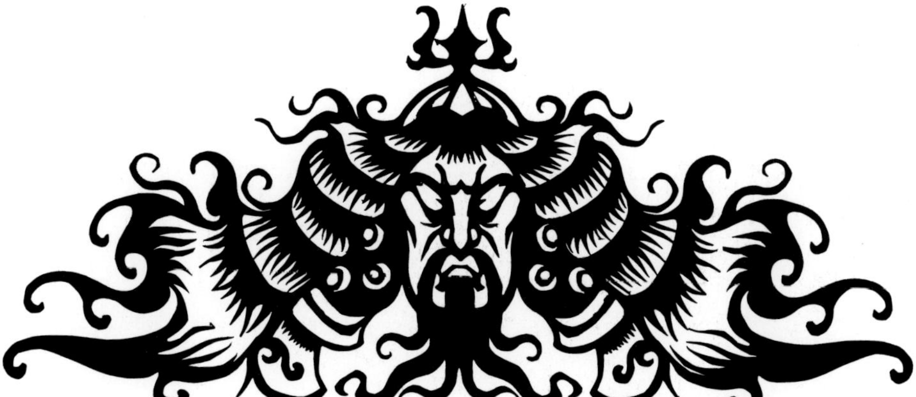

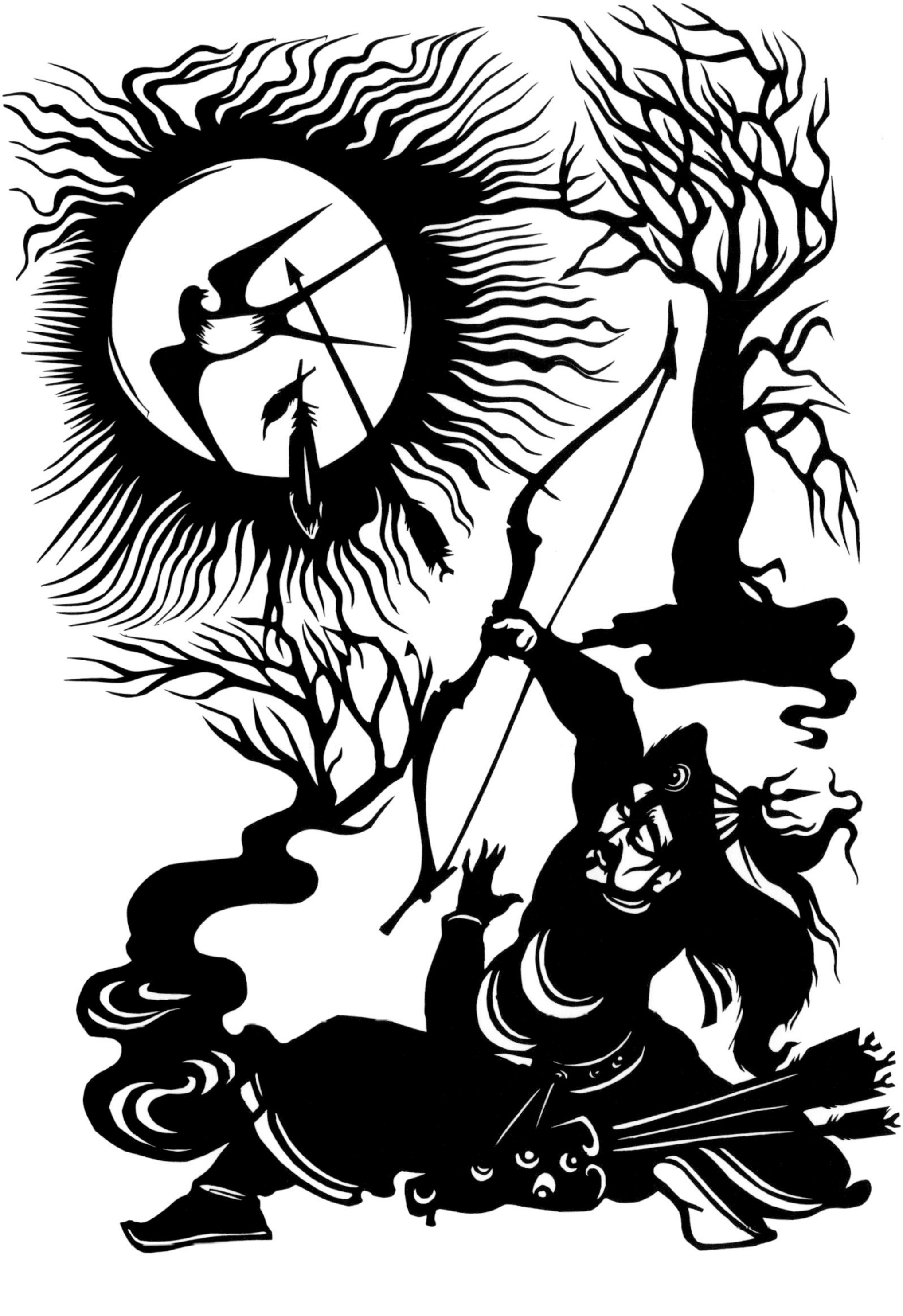

THE LEGEND OF ERKHII MERGEN, THE ARCHER

Once, long ago, seven suns appeared in the sky. The heat of so many fiery suns was so intense that the earth below began to burn. A terrible drought spread over the land. Streams and rivers dried up, and all the plants and trees began to wilt and die. The people of the earth and every living thing suffered terribly from the intolerable heat. Finally, both man and beast began to die.

During these terrible times, there lived a young man named Erkhii Mergen who was famous as the best archer in the world. Erkhii Mergen could shoot an arrow better than anyone and he always hit his target.

The suffering people came in droves to Erkhii Mergen, begging him:

"Erkhii Mergen, help us! Use your skill to shoot down the seven suns, or everything in this world will surely perish!"

Erkhii Mergen was proud of his ability, his strong thumbs, and his immense strength. He was young and fierce and felt ready to take on any foe. In his pride, Erkhii Mergen said to the people:

"Not only will I shoot down the seven suns, but I promise to use only seven arrows to accomplish the deed. If I should not succeed, I swear to you all that I will cut off my thumbs! I will cease to be a man and will become an animal, an animal that never drinks pure water, that eats only last year's dry grass and that lives forever in one of the earth's dark holes!"

The people were grateful to Erkhii Mergen, but wondered at his boundless confidence.

When the suns rose in the east the next morning and began tormenting the earth below, Erkhii Mergen set out to find a spot to do battle. From the summit of a high hill, as the suns passed over his head one by one, the fearless archer drew back his powerful bow, aimed his arrows and let them fly. The twang of Erkhii Mergen's bowstring vibrated over the land as the archer destroyed six of the seven scorching suns with six sharp arrows.

Now taking aim at his final target, Erkhii Mergen let go the seventh and last arrow. At that very moment, a swallow crossed the arrow's path! The arrow ripped the bird's tail, forking it as it remains today. Missing its mark, the arrow fell to the earth.

The seventh sun, seeing how Erkhii Mergen had destroyed its brothers, quickly disappeared in fright behind a western mountain.

Stunned by what had happened, Erkhii Mergen became enraged at the unfortunate swallow and determined to catch and destroy it.

Mounting his loyal piebald horse, he commanded it to give chase. The devoted steed told him:

"Master, our honor is at stake. I will chase that swallow until the sun sets. If my swift legs should not succeed in catching it, then you may cut them off and throw them in the desert, where I shall spend the remainder of my days!"

Erkhii Mergen and his piebald horse thundered across the Mongolian steppe, chasing the swallow for many hours. But no matter how fast it ran, the piebald horse could not capture the bird. Each time the horse got close, the swallow would dart away and avoid being caught, almost as if the bird were mocking the angry horse and its rider.

As the seventh sun began to set and the sky grew red, Erkhii Mergen, now more frustrated than ever, did as the horse demanded: he cut off the animal's forelegs and threw them in the desert. At that moment, the archer's piebald horse changed into a jerboa, a jumping mouse, and it is for this reason that the jerboa's front legs are shorter than its hind legs.

Now Erkhii Mergen kept his boastful but horrible promise to the people. He cut off his thumbs and changed himself from a man into a marmot. He sought out a dark hole deep in the earth and began drinking impure water and eating old grass. If you look at a marmot's claws you will see that they are four, because Erkhii Mergen cut off his own thumbs. In the marmot's body there is a piece of meat that the Mongols call 'man's meat.' This piece was originally Erkhii Mergen's flesh. People ceased eating it out of respect for the archer who saved the world by destroying six scorching suns.

The seventh sun, though it still warms the world, is frightened of Erkhii Mergen. It runs to hide behind the mountains for part of the day, and this is why day and night appear in succession.

Regarding the swallow who got away: its tail is still forked, but when it spies a man riding a horse, it flies to and fro around their heads as if to say:

"You cut my tail, but you can't catch me. Just you try!..."

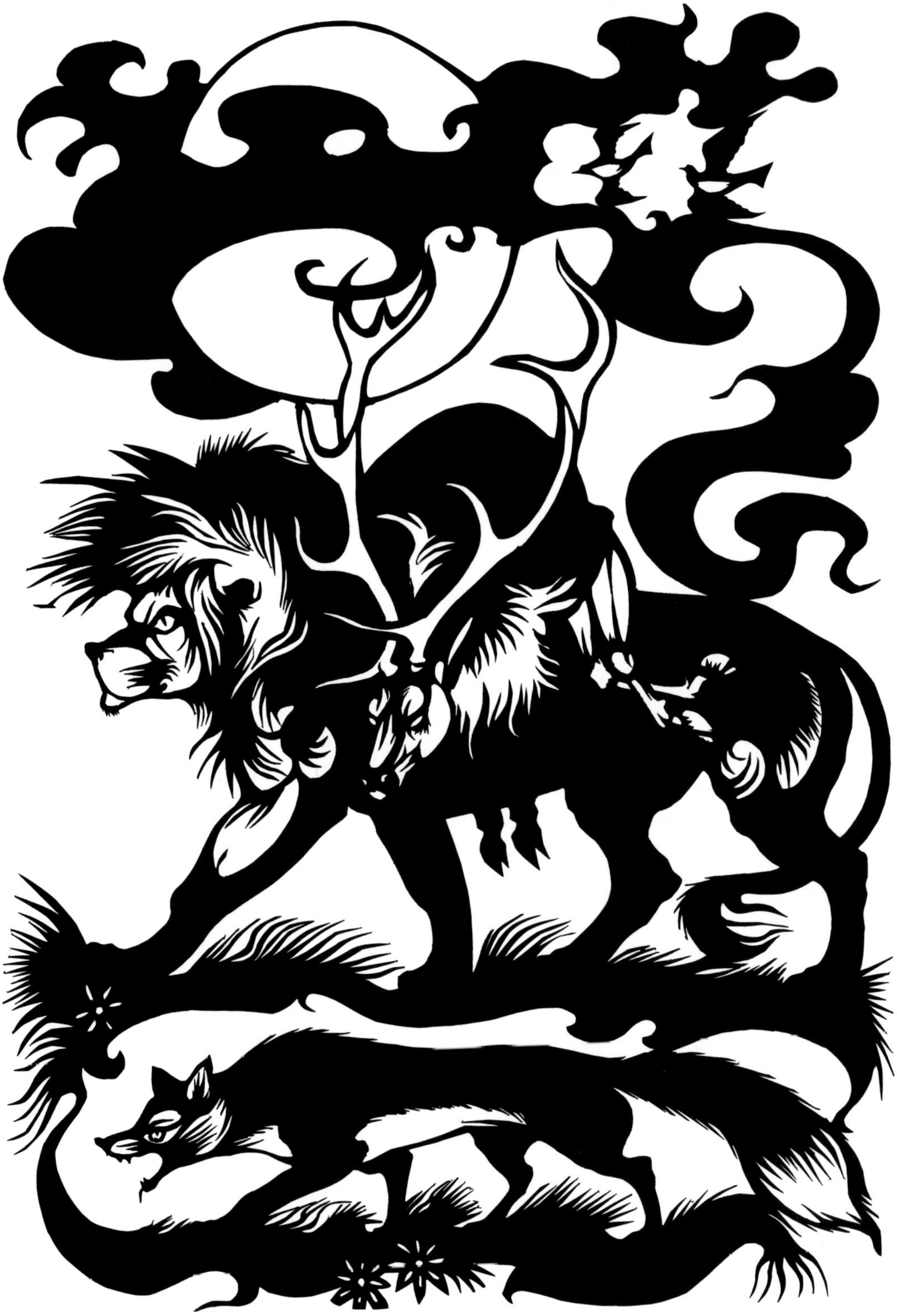

The Fox and the Lion

For many years the Fox and the Lion hunted for their food together. When they caught an unsuspecting victim, they would carry the prize to their cave where they could enjoy their meal undisturbed.

One day, the two hunters caught one of the biggest deer in the forest. The Lion, who until then had always carried the catch, turned to the Fox and said:

"Today it's your turn!"

The Fox, one of the wiliest of creatures as we all know, responded:

"Why, of course I'll carry the deer! With pleasure! But there is one problem. One can't carry this deer without groaning, and groaning is the difficult part. So I'll walk in front with the prey, and you follow and groan."

As the Fox approached the deer to lift it on his back, the Lion paused and thought for a moment. Somehow he did not like the idea of following behind the smaller animal, complaining. After all, he was King of the Beasts and what would all the other animals think to see the King behaving in such a shameful manner? Out of pride, the Lion told the Fox:

"Listen. I've reconsidered the matter. I'll carry the deer and you make the noise."

Hoisting the heavy deer on his back, the proud Lion clenched his teeth and set out. The Fox followed behind groaning loudly, now and then revealing a little smile on his face.

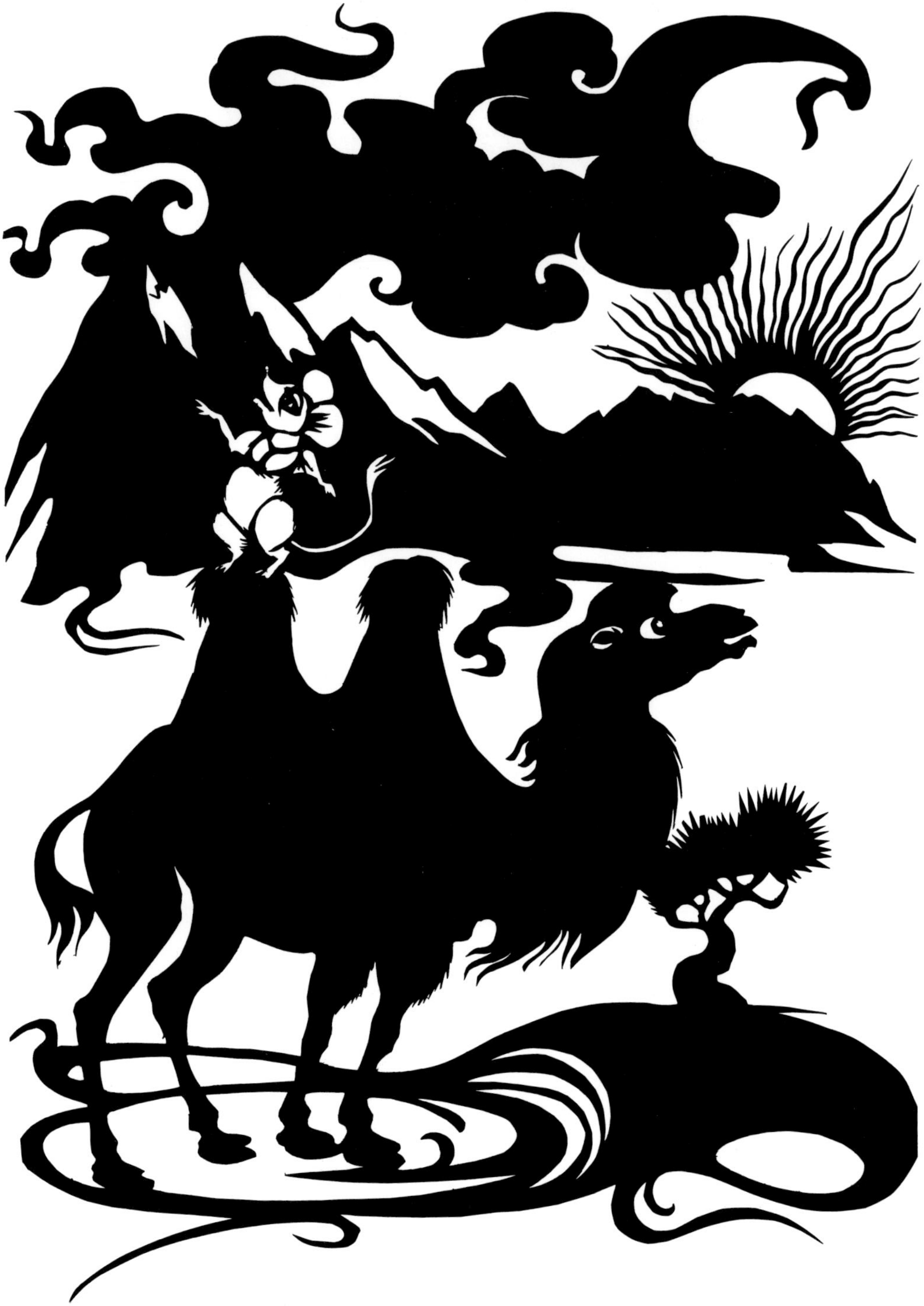

WHY THE CAMEL ROLLS IN THE ASHES

A great many years ago, The Buddha began assigning an animal to each of the years of the twelve-year Mongolian calendar. When He had finished assigning eleven animals, The Buddha paused to consider which animal should be alloted the twelfth and final year.

On hearing this, the Camel and the Mouse, neither of whom had been selected, rushed to see The Buddha. Bowing respectfully before The Great Sage, each presented himself as a worthy candidate. The Buddha listened in silence as each animal argued his case.

When the elaborate pleas came to an end, the Wise Buddha, not wishing to offend either of the eager and equally deserving animals, quietly told the Camel and the Mouse that they would have to resolve the matter themselves in a friendly and honest way.

The big Camel and the tiny Mouse, after much discussion and debate, finally agreed that they would settle the issue with a contest. The first to see the light of the new morning sun the very next day would be the winner, and the winner would enter the twelve-year Mongolian calendar for all time.

That night, in the darkness, in the middle of a wide, open plain, the Camel took up a position facing East. The Mouse, who had asked the Camel if he could sit on his hump, fixed his eyes on a faraway, snow-covered mountain to the West. Eyes propped wide open, the two anxious contestants settled down to wait for the critical moment.

At dawn, when the great fiery ball began its slow ascent, one thin early ray glanced off the snowy western mountaintop. The Mouse squealed out:

"There it is! I see the sun! I win!"

"What?" cried the Camel, who knew that the sun rose in the East. "Why, you little sneak! You've cheated! You'll pay for this!"

As the terrified Mouse scurried down the Camel's hump to seek safety in a nearby pile of ashes, the Camel charged after him. He threw his heavy body on the ground, and rolled back and forth on the ash pile, hoping to crush the Mouse with his weight.

The Camel didn't squash the Mouse that time, but he's certain that one day he will. Whenever he spies a pile of ashes, he thinks the Mouse must be hiding inside. He snorts, stamps his feet, then lies down and rolls around and around, trying to flatten his tricky little foe.

So it happened that the little Mouse entered the twelve-year Mongolian calendar while the big Camel was excluded.

Feeling sorry for the Camel, the Wise Buddha told him gently that he would never be forgotten. No, in fact the Camel would be represented in the Mongolian calendar by possessing one feature of each of the twelve different animals.

If you look carefully at the Camel, you will see that The Buddha has kept His word, because the Camel has:

> the ears of the Mouse
> the stomach of the Cow
> the paws of the Tiger
> the nose of the Hare
> the body of the Dragon
> the eyes of the Snake
> the mane of the Horse
> the wool of the Sheep
> the hump of the Ape
> the head-crest of the Rooster
> the crooked back-legs of the Dog
> and the tail of the Pig.

This, as you can imagine, makes him a very happy Camel indeed.

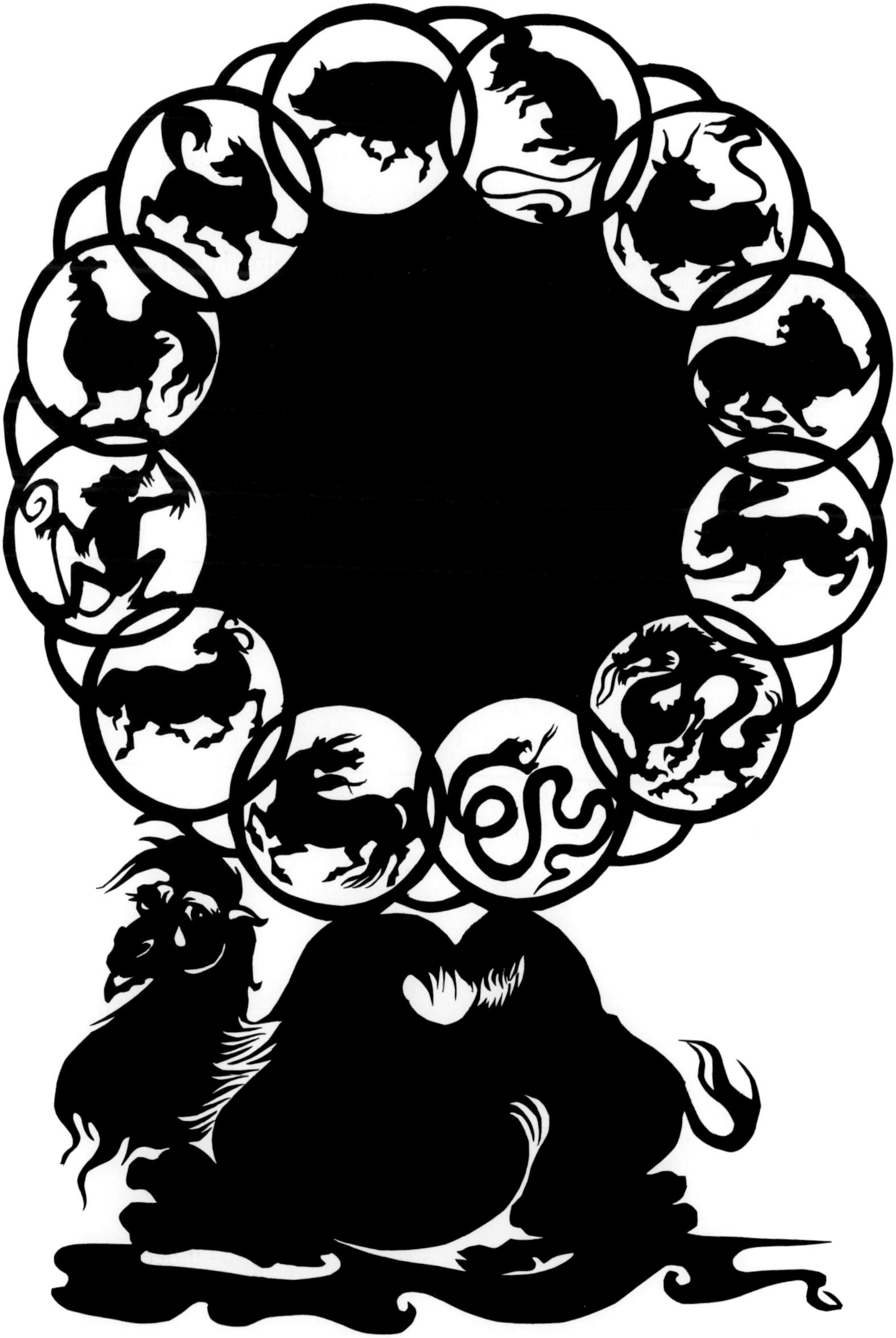

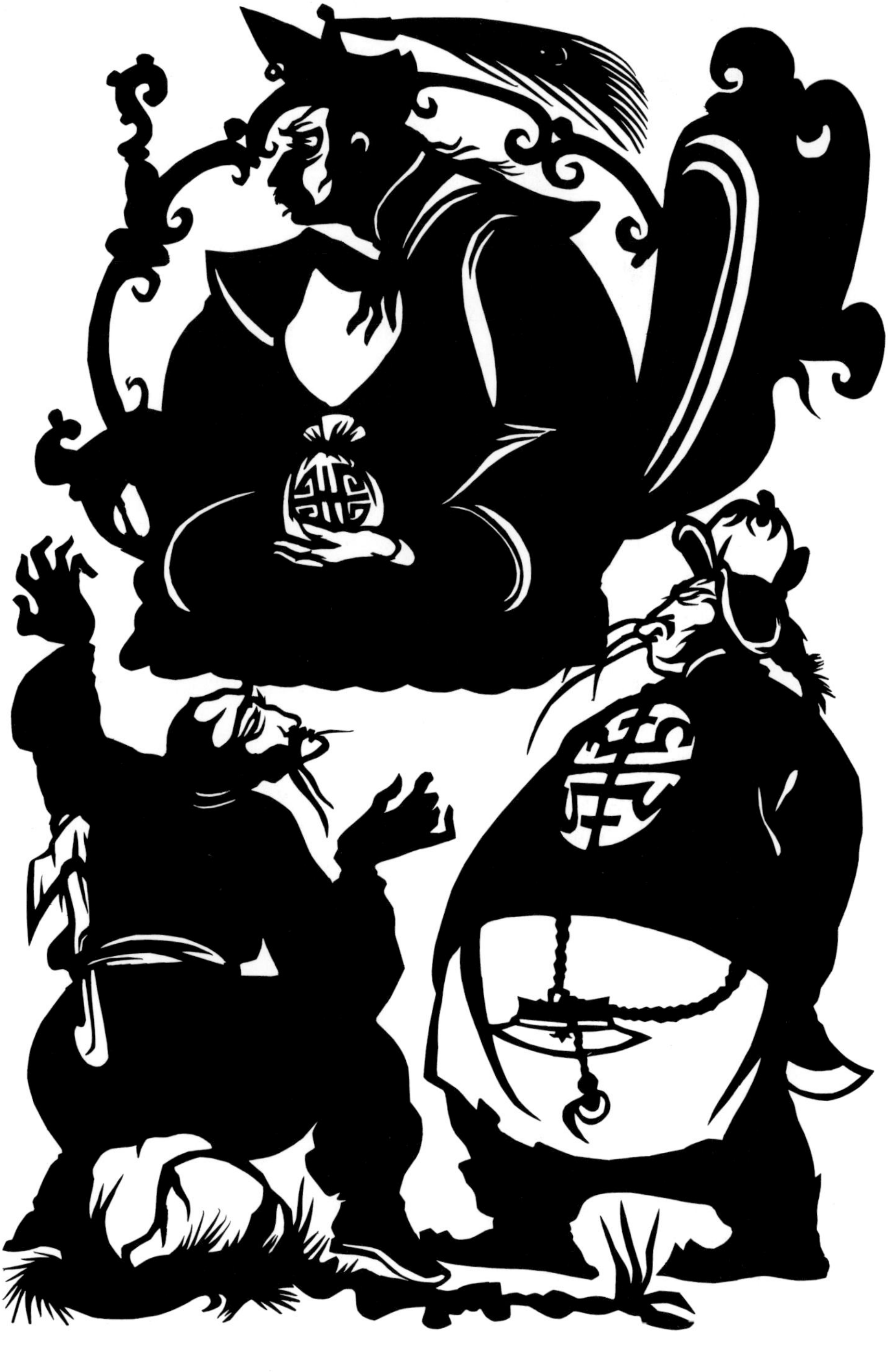

THE WISE JUDGE

There was once a very rich Mongolian herdsman who owned so many of the 'five noble animals' that he was unable to count them all. This Herdsman possessed thousands of sheep and goats, hundreds and hundreds of cattle, and score upon score of camels. On the fastest of his many horses, he always rode on an elegant Mongol saddle, made of finely-worked leather and silver, and on the belt of his crimson velvet *del** was to be seen the most magnificent silver knife and flint in all the land.

The Herdsman's *ger** was filled with brightly painted furniture and intricately-stitched felt carpets and his well-fed family wore only garments of the finest imported Chinese silks. The wife—well, the wife! She was covered with so much splendid Mongolian silver jewelry decorated with corals and other precious stones that she fairly shone in the sun and could hardly move. Yes indeed, this Herdsman was very wealthy, but he could never have enough and he was also very greedy.

One day, as the Herdsman was returning from Sunday Market, a weekly fair where people came from all over the region to barter, trade, and make merry, he lost his wallet. Inside the wallet was the money the Herdsman had made that day: one million *tugrik*.* The wallet lay in the dirt by the roadside and was soon found by two poor but honest men who immediately took it to the District Judge and explained what had happened.

When the Greedy Rich Herdsman discovered that his wallet was missing he lost his appetite and became quite feverish. He rushed to the District Judge to report his loss. As soon as he entered the Judge's office and saw his wallet on the Judge's desk, he grabbed it and stuffed it in his *del*, sighing with relief.

The surprised Judge exclaimed: "Just a moment, Sir. Why have you taken that wallet from my desk without my permission? Is the wallet yours?"

The Greedy Rich Herdsman hastily replied: "Of course it's mine! I lost it and now I've found it!"

The Judge then said: "Well, Sir. If this wallet really is yours, and you are so relieved at finding it again, you should give a reward to the man who found it and brought it here, in gratitude for his honesty."

Now he began questioning the Herdsman. "How many *tugrik* were in the wallet when you lost it?"

The Greedy Rich Herdsman's face changed color at the prospect of parting with some of his money for a reward. He imagined that the Judge himself wanted reward money, so he said without batting an eye: "When I lost my wallet it had two million *tugrik* in it!"

Taking the wallet from his *del*, he counted the money. With a shocked look on his face, the Greedy Rich Herdsman announced: "What's this? There are only one million *tugrik* here! Whoever found my wallet probably took the other million for himself! The finder has already been rewarded!"

Then the Judge asked the Herdsman: "Ah, good Sir, now I understand. That means you were going to give a reward of a million *tugrik* to the man who found your wallet, weren't you?"

The Greedy Rich Herdsman replied boastfully: "Our family has always been well off. Of course, Your Honor, I would gladly have given one million *tugrik* as a reward to the man that found this precious wallet of mine!"

The Judge then said: "Well, Sir, this wallet cannot be yours because there were only one million *tugrik* in it when it was found, not two million. There is a witness to the truth of this because two men, not one, found it. This wallet must belong to someone else. If you begin searching for your own wallet now, you might still find your two million *tugrik*. You may go now. I wish you luck."

Hearing the Judge speak with such reason, the Rich Herdsman decided to tell the truth to try to extricate himself from this predicament.

"Dear Judge," he cried. "I lied just now! This wallet with only one million *tugrik* in it really is mine. When I saw that my wallet had already been found and turned in, I had the evil idea that I might save myself the reward money. I lied when I said there were two million *tugrik* in the wallet. And I wrongly blamed the finder for having already taken the reward!"

The Herdsman told the whole truth to the Judge, begging for his pardon. But the Judge did not like the Herdsman's low cunning, his greed, his lies, and his attempt to blame the honest finders for stealing. The Judge decided that the Greedy Rich Herdsman needed a hard lesson.

"Sir, since you were going to give the finders of your wallet one million *tugrik* as a reward, do it now. You may take your empty wallet home with the memory of your lesson. In the future, try to be less greedy and deceitful and more generous and honest."

The Greedy Rich Herdsman stuffed his empty wallet in his *del* and stalked out of the Judge's office in a rage, never to be heard from again.

Meanwhile, the fame of the Wise Judge spread far and wide.

Del: the Mongolian national dress. A del is a wraparound sort of coat made of silk, velvet or simpler fabrics, belted and fastened with silver buttons. In winter, the del is lined with sheep's wool for warmth.

Known as a yurt in the West, the ger is the national dwelling of the Mongolians. It is a round structure made of pounded felt and covered in white canvas, which is moved according to the herding seasons.

Tugrik: the Mongolian currency. As of 1996, one US dollar equals roughly five hundred tugrik. The Greedy Rich Herdsman in this story would have had about $2,500 in his wallet.

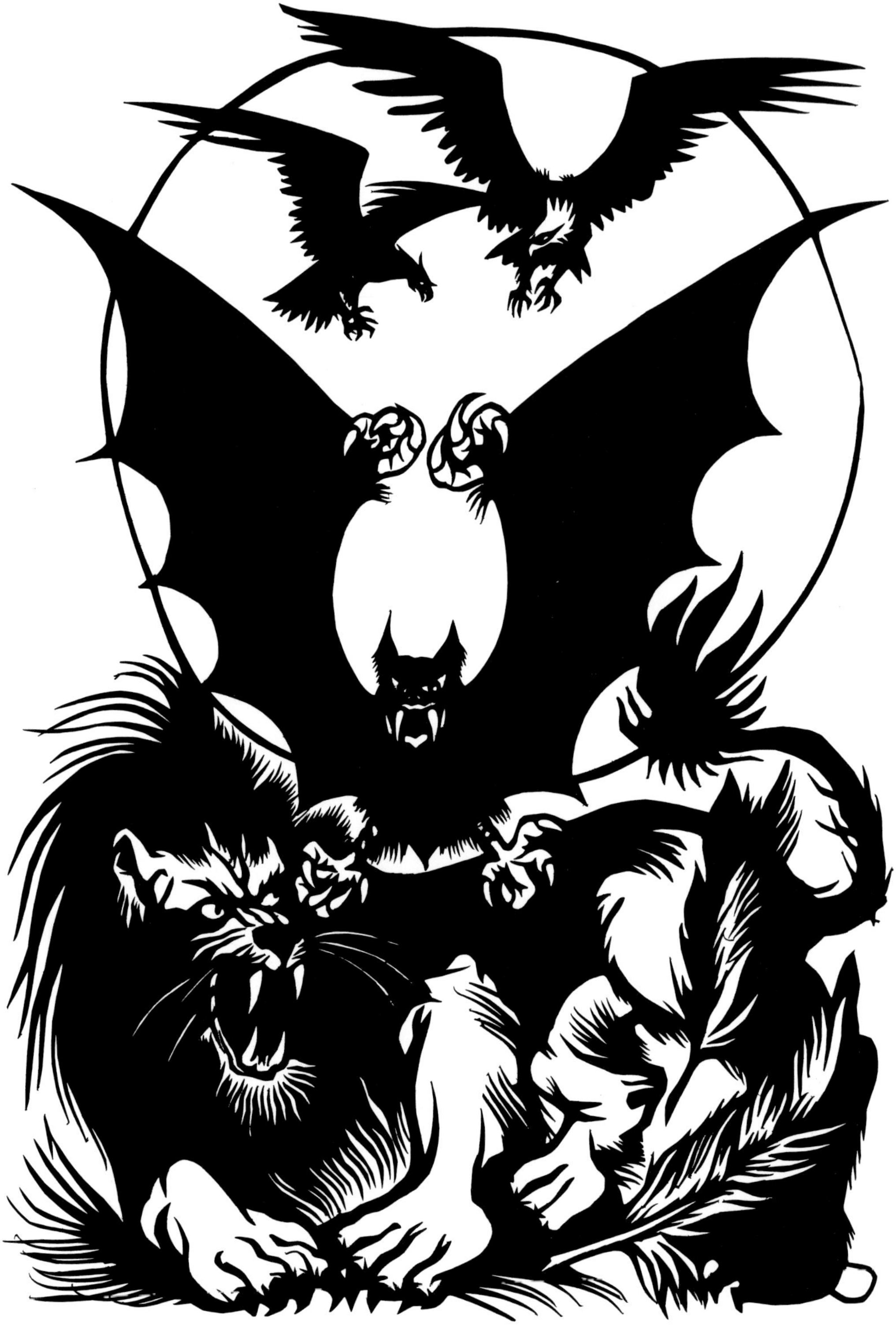

Why the Bat Lives in the Dark

Once, a long time ago, a terrible battle broke out between the Birds and the Beasts of this Earth. No one remembers any more what caused this battle to start, but the fighting was so ferocious that the whole earth shook and the land was covered with broken feathers, bloody hair, and the bodies of fallen creatures.

On one side of the battle swarmed the animals of the air. All the birds, great and small, were massed in the heavens, from the most powerful eagle, sharp-eyed hawk, and swift falcon to the tiniest finch and fragile sparrow. Opposing the birds were formidable adversaries: the kingly lion, menacing tiger, mighty stag, massive bear, and all the other beasts of the land.

The only animal in the whole world that did not choose sides in this war was the Bat. As a mouse with wings or a birdy beast, the Bat gambled on its dual nature, waiting to see which side would win. In this way, when the time came, it could claim victory with the conquering army.

When it looked as though the birds of the air were gaining the advantage, the Bat would become like a bird, flap its wings and screech:

"I'm a bird, too! I'll peck at the beasts below, pierce their skins, and dig my sharp talons into their flesh! Forward to battle, birds!"

But when the tide of the great battle shifted, and suddenly it seemed as though the beasts would win, the Bat would hide its wings and flash its mouselike grin. Baring its sharp teeth, it would bark:

"Beware! I am a dangerous beast! C'mon beasts! Let's attack the birds and bite them till they fall from the sky! Hooray for the beasts!"

As the battle raged on and on, both the birds and the beasts displayed courage in their terrible fight, never ceasing for a moment to give their best for the sake of their cause. After many weeks of struggle, however, it became clear to everyone that both sides were evenly matched, that neither side would ever be able to overcome the other. And so the birds and the beasts agreed to cease fighting. They declared a truce.

In the quiet that followed, both armies counted their dead, collected their wounded, and called out the names of their brothers, sisters, and friends who might not have perished on the battlefield.

No one called the name of the Bat. No one wanted the one who had darted from one camp to the other throughout the long war, not knowing where it belonged, telling false things to each army in turn.

The animals had seen it fighting like this, first on one side, then on the other side of the battlefield. They were angry. Neither the birds nor the beasts would now, or ever, agree to claim the Bat as one of their own. Instead, for its disloyalty, they banished the Bat from their midst.

The sorry Bat, a traitor to both birds and beasts, was now ashamed of its behavior during the feud. It curled up its mousy body and took flight. Seeking out a remote corner of the world, it entered the recesses of Mother Earth and concealed itself in her black and silent caves, venturing out only at night in search of food.

From that day, the Bat has made its home in the dark, wrapped against the dampness in its leathery cloak, living out the life of a lonely outcast.

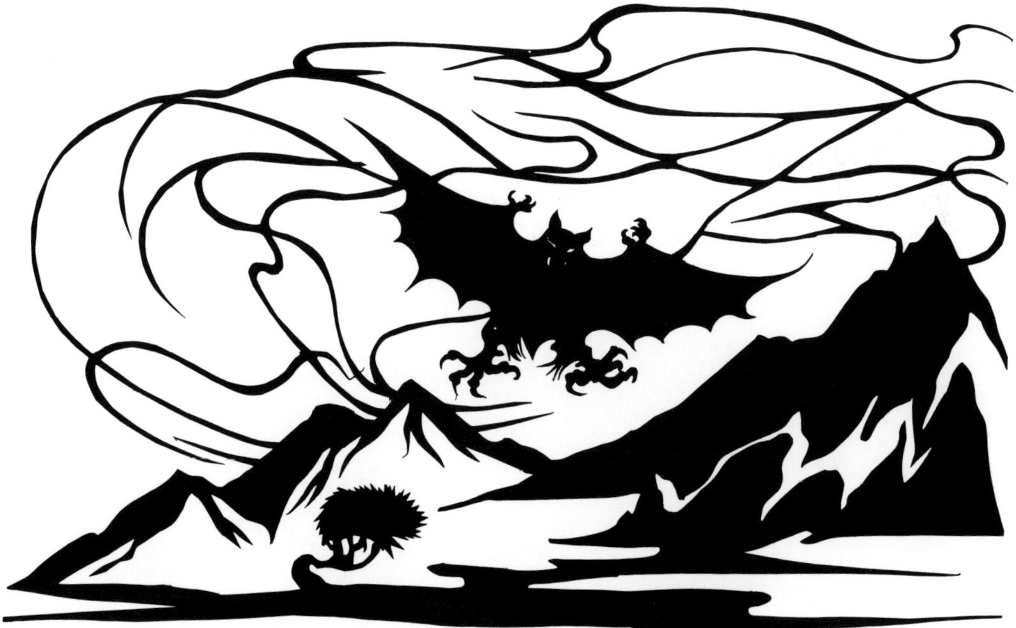

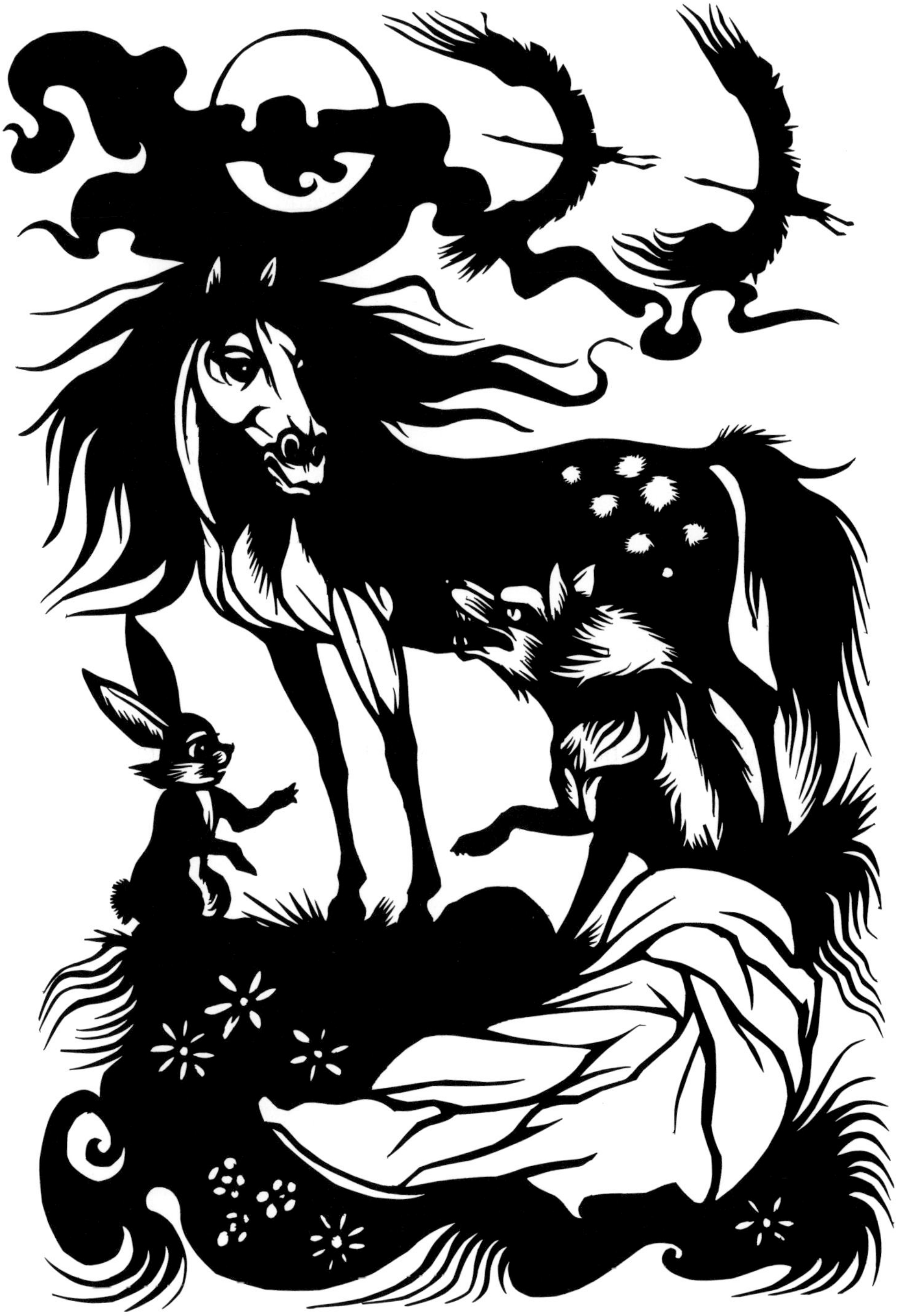

How a Small Rabbit Saved a Large Horse

Once upon a time two brother horses were born on the wide rolling steppes of Central Mongolia.

While they were still young they were sold to a man who lived in the west, near the cold, snowy Altai mountains, far from their home

After many years of serving their master well, the two horses, old and weary, began to dream about their native steppe. They longed to eat its sweet grasses one last time. They finally decided to run away and find their home.

On the long and arduous journey, the elder of the two horses became so tired and lame that he began to lag behind his younger brother. At last he was unable to go a step further. Sighing, he lay down for the last time by the side of the road.

"Brother," he said. "I cannot go on. You must continue home without me. As your elder, I will give you three pieces of advice for a safe journey. First, do not take any paths. Always keep to the main roads. Second, do not be curious—do not approach anything that you cannot clearly see. Third, do not unwrap anything that is already wrapped up."

So saying, the older horse gave the younger his blessing and closed his eyes to sleep.

The younger brother now set out on his own and, as younger brothers often do, immediately forgot the advice of his older sibling.

After walking along the main road under a hot sun for some hours, he came across a path that cut over the mountains through a forest. Ignoring the first piece of advice, the younger horse said to himself:

"I'll bet this path will get me home sooner. And it will be so much cooler walking under the trees."

The shaded path did indeed wind over the mountain. On the other side, it led onto an open plain. Far ahead, as the track almost disappeared in the distance, the Horse spied an indistinct brown object. Wondering what it could be in such a remote spot and forgetting his brother's second warning, he galloped towards it.

Coming up close, the younger brother discovered that the object was a securely tied sack, with something large inside that appeared to be moving. Curious to find out what was trapped in such a big bag, he quickly unfastened the rope.

Out of the sack sprang a large, angry Wolf, one that was clearly ravenously hungry. With yellow eyes fixed on the Horse, the Wolf snarled:

"So! You came back! You're the horse that chased me down when I was eating sheep! When your owner trapped me, he tied me up in this bag and left me to rot! If it hadn't been for you, I would have escaped! Now, I'm going to eat you!"

"Wait a minute," cried the astonished and terrified Horse. "I'm not that horse! I just got here! Didn't you notice I just freed you from this sack?"

"You're lying," screamed the Wolf. "You look exactly like that fast horse!"

Just as the Wolf was about to pounce on the trembling Horse and eat it, up hopped a Rabbit.

"Hey there!" he yelled, "what's going on between you two?"

Wolf and Horse each told the long-eared animal his own version of the story. The Rabbit, who knew all about hungry wolves, believed the Horse and quickly thought of a plan to save the innocent animal. He said:

"Well, Mr. Wolf, that's an interesting story, but it's really hard for me to believe that a big, strong fellow such as yourself was trapped in such a little bag. Are you telling the truth? Because if you are, I'll not only let you eat Mr. Horse but, as a reward, I'll give you myself to eat as well!"

"What?" cried the Wolf. "You don't believe me?"

"With all due respect, Mr. Wolf," the Rabbit replied, "I simply cannot believe that you fit in that sack until I see it with my own eyes."

To prove he was telling the truth, the Wolf jumped back into the sack. Since his head was still uncovered, the Rabbit exclaimed:

"Mr. Wolf, it seems you are indeed too big for that sack—your head doesn't fit inside!"

Whereupon the Wolf, eager to prove himself and to eat both Horse and Rabbit, drew the sack up over his head.

Before the Wolf knew what had happened, the quick little Rabbit sprang forward, tied the opening tight and trapped the Wolf in the sack once more. The Horse neighed with admiration and glee, and the two animals ran off laughing to safety.

Thanking the Rabbit, the younger-brother horse continued on his journey. Now carefully following his older brother's advice, he arrived safely in his beloved rolling steppes and there lived happily for many, many years.

In this way, and in spite of his size, a small resourceful Rabbit saved a large, old Horse.

As for the Wolf, well, as far as we know, that mean old mangy animal is still trapped and howling inside the sack.

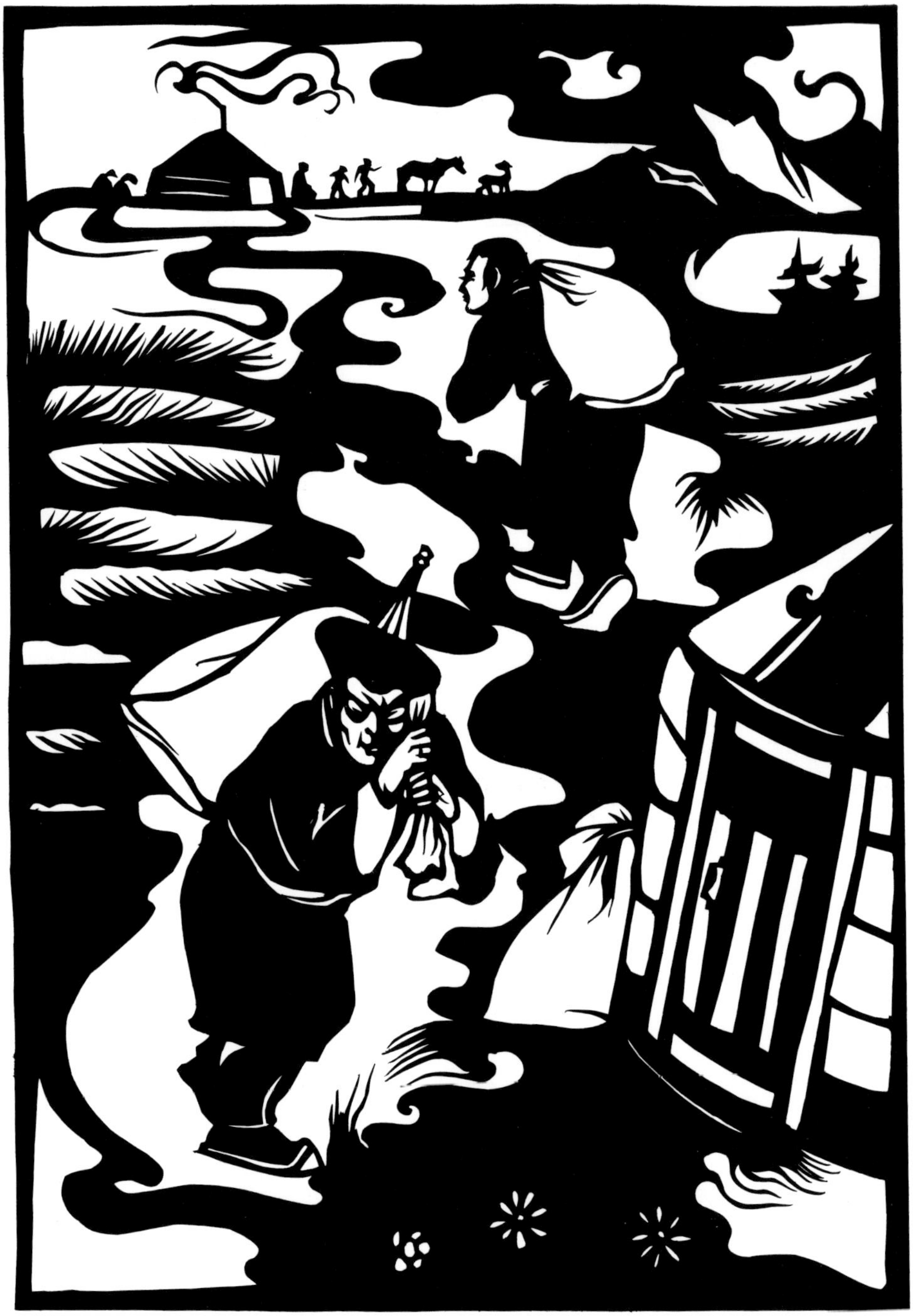

The Two Good Brothers

In the fertile plains of Selenge province, there once lived two brothers who worked hard together growing crops for a living.

The elder of the two brothers lived alone, but the younger had a wife and seven small children.

Year in and year out the brothers toiled side by side, living harmoniously and growing prosperous. Every year when the crops were brought in, they divided the harvest evenly between them.

One afternoon in autumn, when the brothers had finished tying the last bag of grain for the season and gone home to rest, the elder brother sat smoking his pipe on the threshold of his *ger*. He was thinking:

"Has sharing our harvest all these years been the right or the wrong thing to do? My good brother has many children to feed, and I have none. As his family is large, he certainly needs more bread than I do. I think I should give him one more sack of grain!"

That night, while the younger brother slept, the elder brother added another sack of grain to his pile.

The same night, the younger brother lay awake thinking. He was so disturbed that he couldn't sleep, so he awakened his good wife and said to her:

"My dear, I have been thinking over something for a long time. I don't believe we have been doing the right thing all these years, that is, to share our harvest evenly with my brother. He lives alone and has no one to help him with his housework at the end of the day. Let us give him one more sack of grain. He needs it more than we do."

The wife agreed. In the early morning hours when the elder brother was still asleep, the husband and wife lifted a heavy sack of grain onto the elder brother's stocks.

The next day when both brothers awakened, breakfasted, and went to inspect their stores, each was surprised to see that his sacks numbered exactly the same as before. They did not say a word to each other. They scratched their heads, puzzled, and went to work as usual.

The next night the elder brother tried again to increase his brother's stockpile, but the younger brother figured out what he had done and put the sack back in the wee hours of the morning.

In the end, it was no use: the two good brothers realized how much each wanted to help the other. They realized how devoted and loving they were and they simply carried on as before.

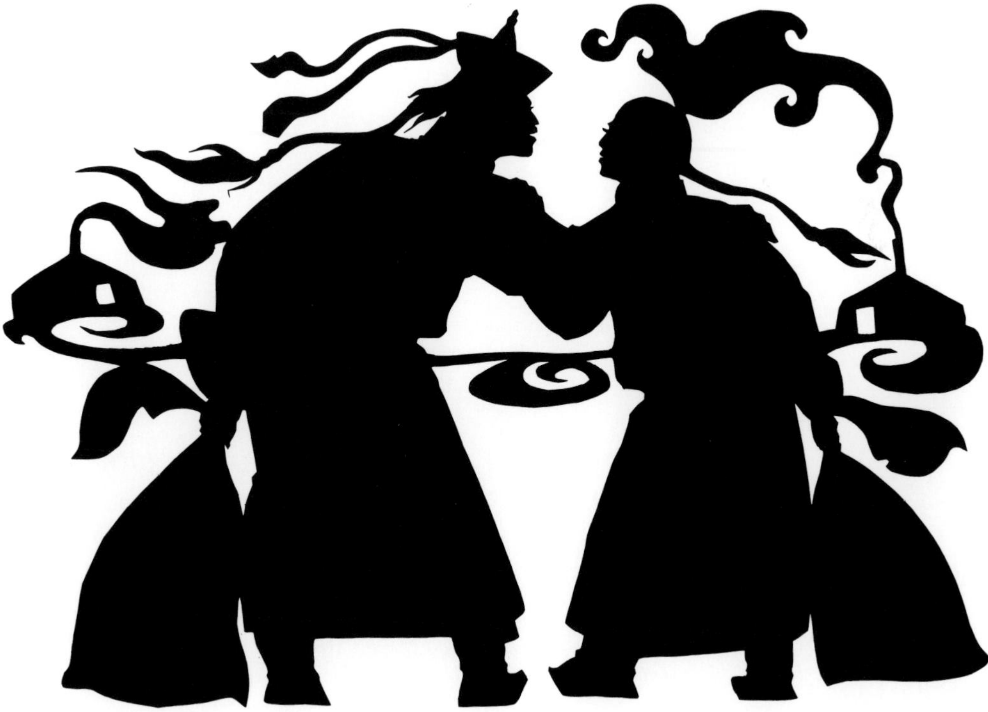

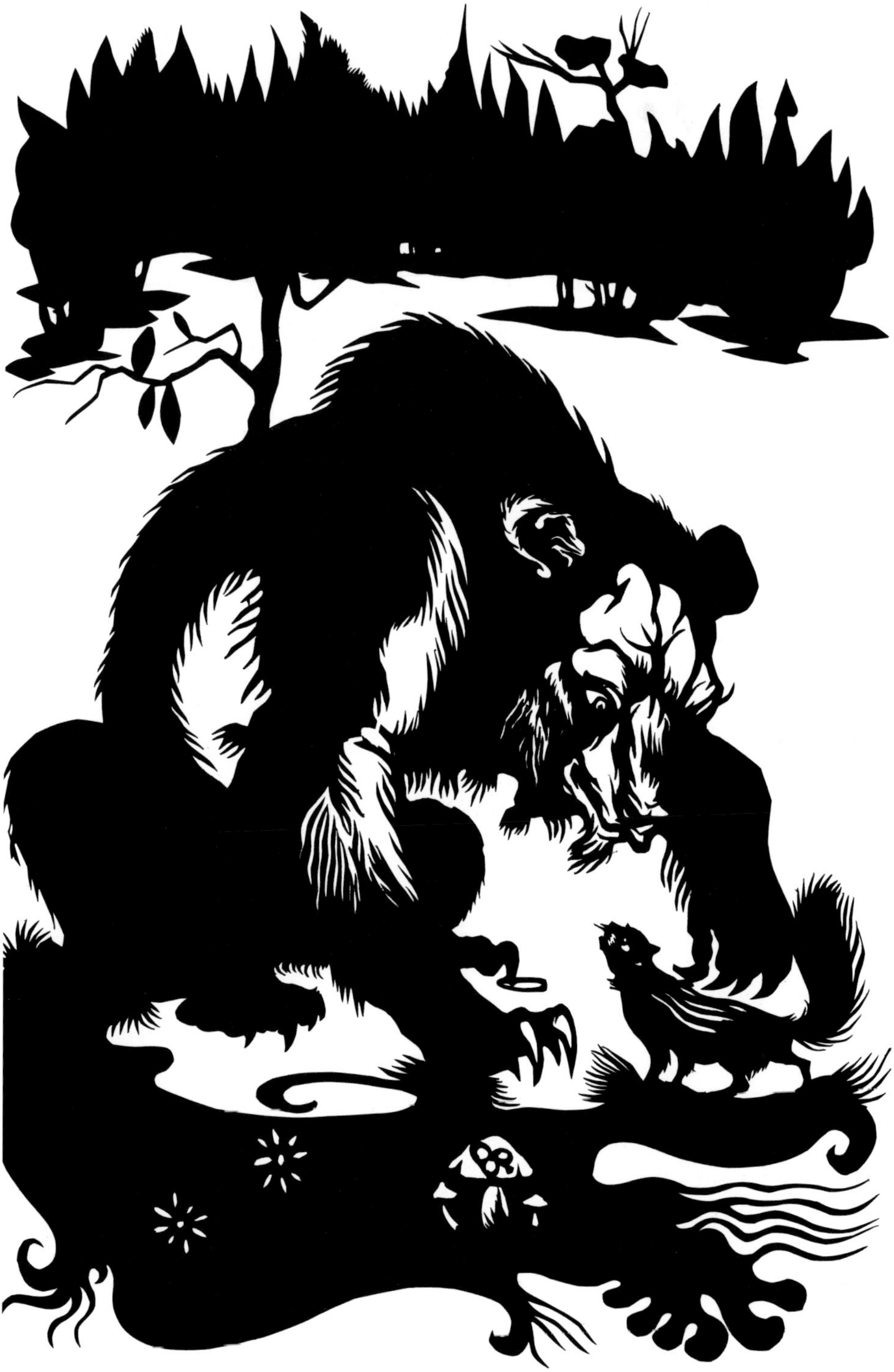

HOW THE CHIPMUNK GOT ITS STRIPES

Do you know why the Chipmunk has stripes on its back? I'll tell you the story.

After a long, snowy Winter, Spring began to arrive at last. As the days grew warmer, the Bear awakened from its sleep and with effort crawled out of its dark den. The Bear had grown thin during the winter and could hardly stand on its big paws. Having eaten nothing for months, he was extremely hungry. But what to do? There was still nothing to eat, no green grass, no berries and certainly no honey, which we all know how much bears love. The ground was still frozen so that the Bear couldn't even dig roots.

What to do? Who could the Bear ask for a bit of food to fill his empty belly? The Bear thought and thought.

"I know," he cried. "I'll ask the resourceful little Chipmunk!"

He set out to find his tiny friend.

Lumbering through the forest, the Bear called out this way and that. After a thorough search and much inquiry, sure enough, a squeaky voice called back:

"Hey, Mr. Bear! So you're awake again and ready to greet the Spring! But oh my, just look at you! How thin you've grown these past months!"

"Yes, my friend," the Bear replied, "it's true. Here I am again, but I'm as hungry as a...as a bear! You are such a good and thrifty fellow. Could you possibly give me something to fill my empty belly? I would be so grateful."

You can see for yourselves how friendly chipmunks can be just by watching them scurry up and down those big trees, looking at you with that twinkle in their eyes. The Chipmunk was pleased and flattered that the big Bear had come to it first to ask for food. The tiny creature led the bear immediately to its well-stocked pantry. There the Bear found piles of cedar nuts that the Chipmunk had carefully collected the previous autumn. You may not know this, but bears love cedar nuts at least as much as honey.

The delighted, ravenous Bear took pawfuls of these delicious nuts to fill his growling stomach as the happy host looked on.

When a bear has a full belly, it is especially friendly and can be quite affectionate. In gratitude for this satisfying meal, the Bear picked up the Chipmunk to thank it, and began caressing its furry body with a huge paw.

"Thank you, little friend! You have been more generous with your food than I imagined!"

With one final long stroke of its paw, the Bear let the Chipmunk go. As you know, some creatures are not aware of their own strength, and the Bear was unaware that its sharp claws had scratched the little Chipmunk's back, leaving long lines on its body.

From that day to this, five dark stripes have remained on the back of the tiny Chipmunk, marks of its generosity to the big and hungry—but grateful—Bear.

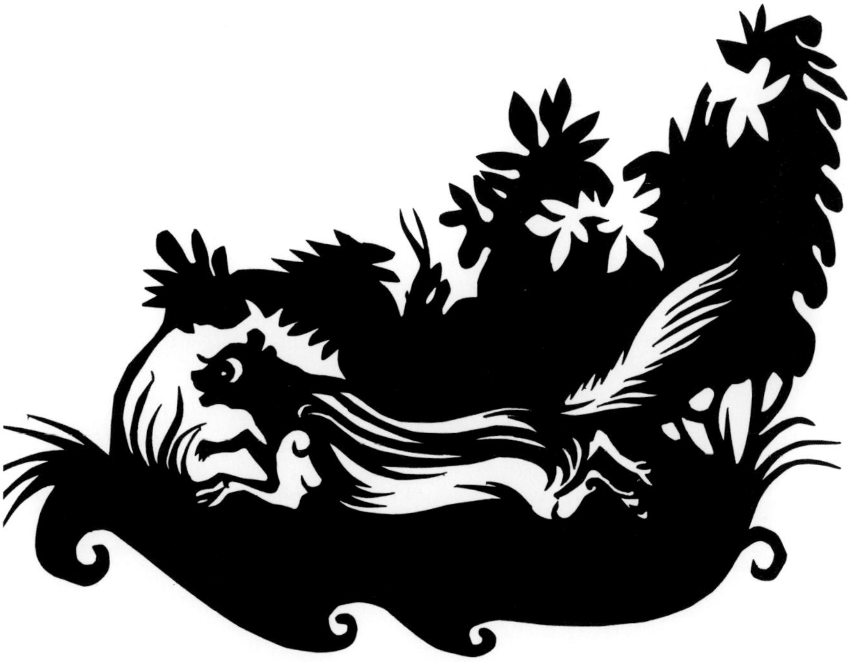

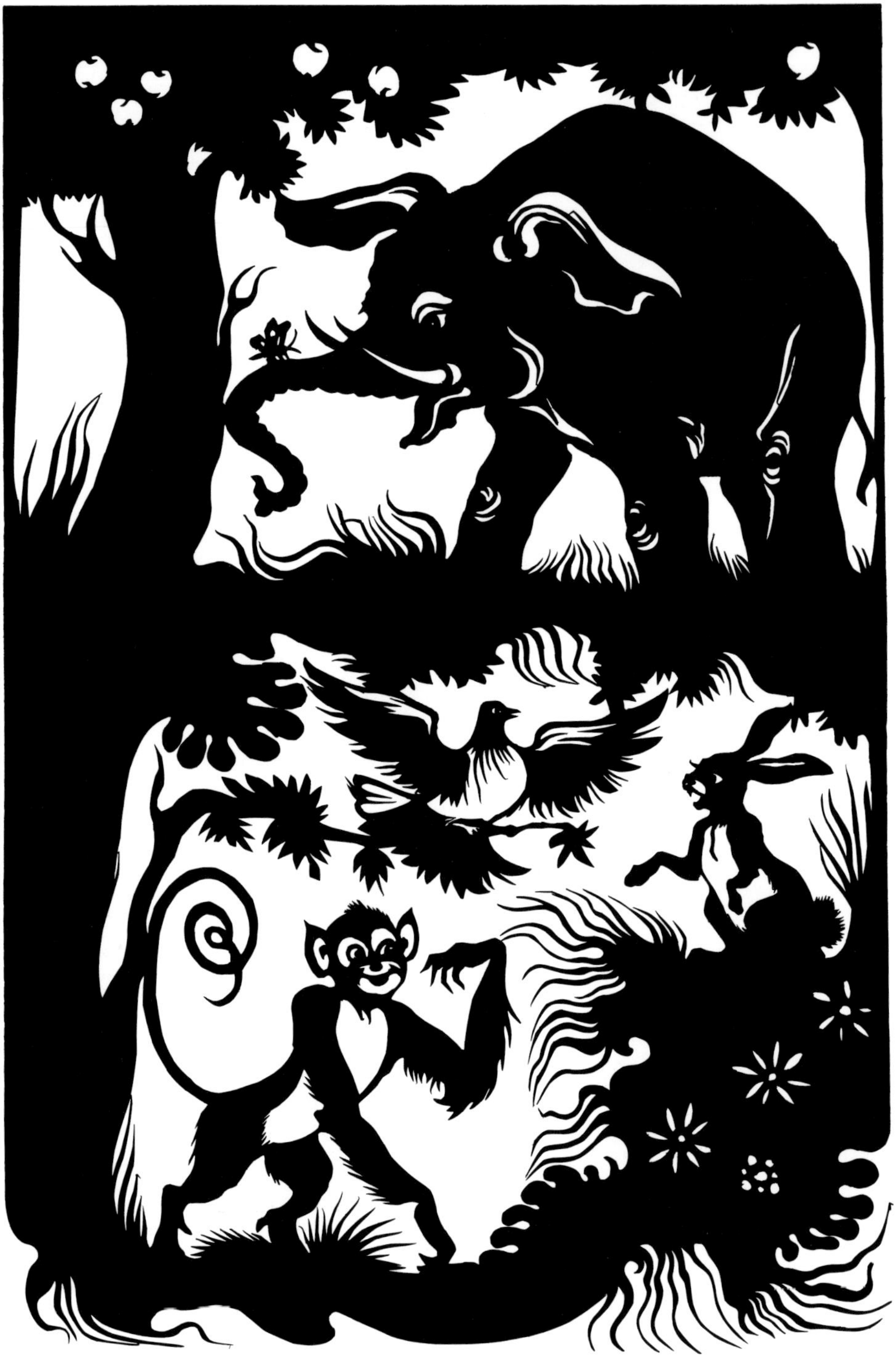

The Four Friendly Animals

Once upon a time, in a beautiful forest in India, lived a Dove, a Hare, a Monkey, and an Elephant. One day, after discussing the matter carefully, they agreed:

"Since we all live together in such a friendly way, we should respect the oldest among us. The younger ones must listen to whatever he says, serve him and do whatever he wishes."

They all agreed that this was an excellent idea and set about to determine who among them was the oldest.

Near the place where they were discussing this important idea stood an old and very large tree. The Elephant pointed to the tree and said:

"When I was an elephant-calf, I used to rub myself against that tree. At that time the tree and I were the same size."

The Monkey was next to speak. It said:

"When I was little, that tree lacked a single branch on which I might jump and play. The tree was the same size as I was then, and its shade was scarcely large enough to cover me."

It was the Hare's turn to speak. It said:

"When I was little, the tree's roots were just beginning to grow, and I used to dig down in the earth so that I could eat them."

The Dove was the last to speak. It said:

"When I was little, I was pecking at the fallen fruit of a tree and the seeds fell where the tree we are all talking about now stands."

So the Four Friendly Animals discovered that the oldest among them was the Dove, the next oldest the Hare, next the Monkey, and the youngest was the Elephant.

Since they had all agreed to respect the eldest, the Elephant, as the youngest, carried the Monkey on its back. The Monkey carried the Hare on its back, and the oldest, the Dove, rode on top. Being up so high, the Dove was able to reach the fruits of the trees and hand them down to the others.

In this way, the Four Friendly Animals mutually respected, protected and helped one another, and lived together in harmony happily ever after.

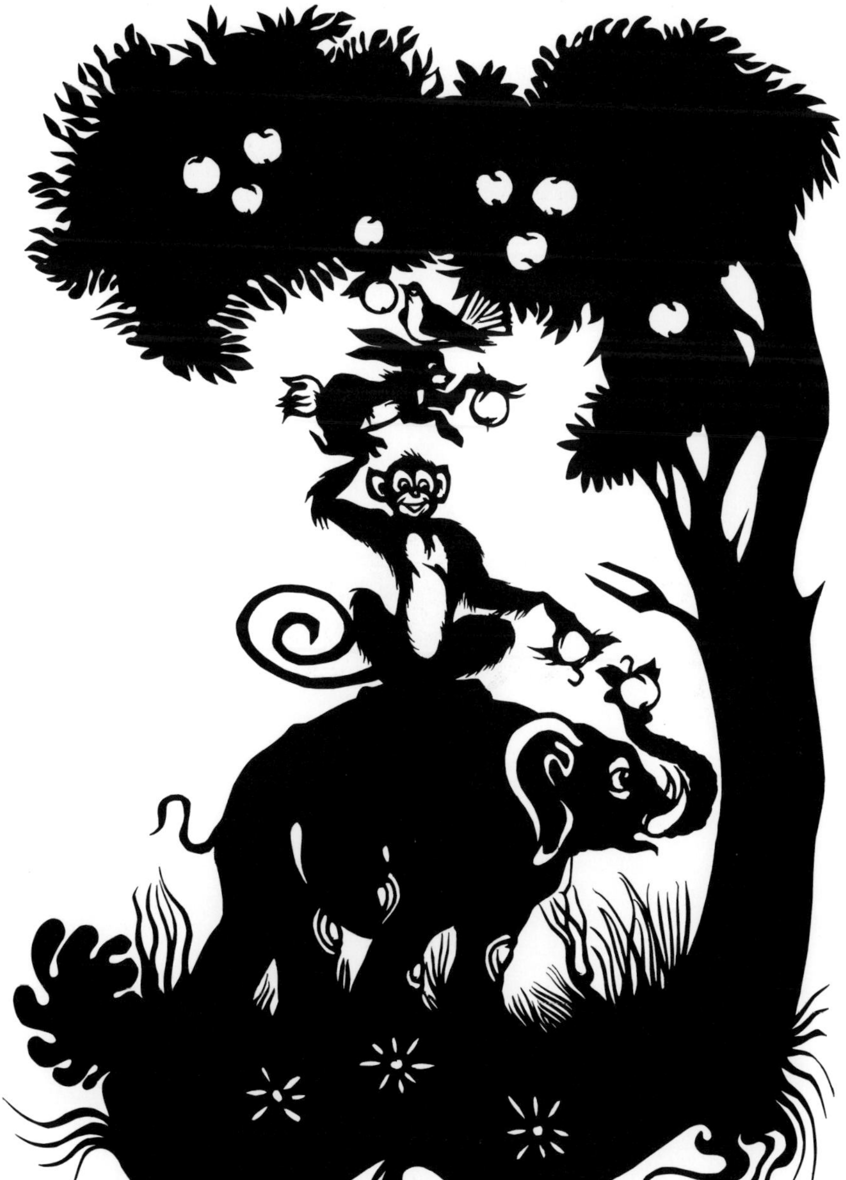

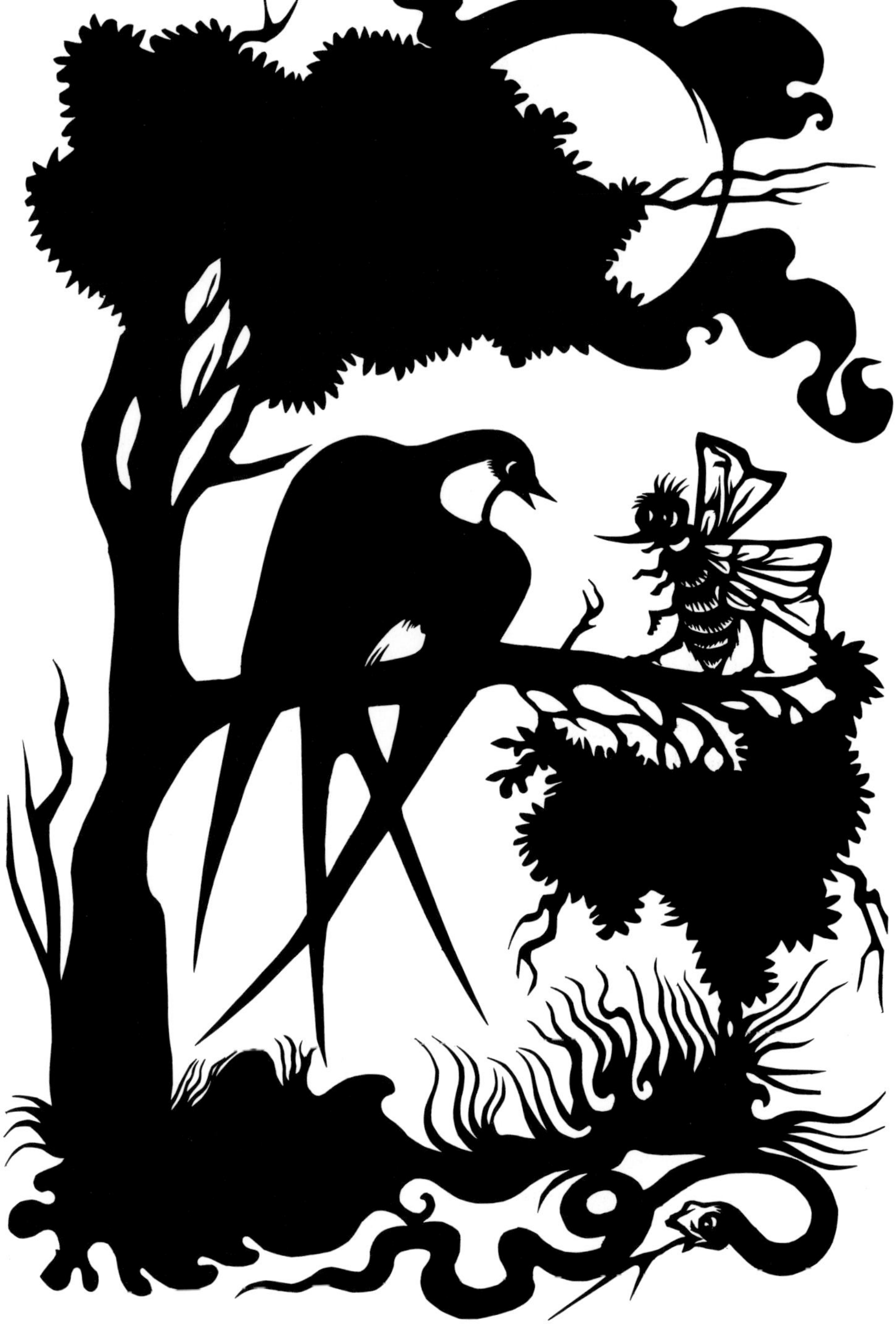

How the Wasp Lost Its Voice

A long time ago, Khan-Garid,* King of the Feathered World, sent for a Swallow and a Wasp. After they had bowed before him, the Khan said: "I command the two of you to fly around the world tomorrow and seek out the animal with the tastiest meat. I will eat only that animal in the future. Return by nightfall with your news!"

Early the next morning, the Swallow and the Wasp set out on their important quest, each flying off in a different direction. As the sun rose higher, the day became warm, bright and beautiful. The Swallow sang as it soared through the blue skies, just happy to be alive, and soon forgot Khan-Garid's command altogether.

In the meantime, on the other side of the world, the harmful Wasp was carrying out the Khan's orders. Leaving a trail of painful stings in its wake, the Wasp methodically tasted the blood of every creature it came across.

As the day drew to a close and the sun began its descent, the two royal emissaries met before the palace of the Khan-Garid to exchange their news. The Swallow, having played away the entire day, was now worried about the Khan's wrath. Hoping that the Wasp had discovered the tastiest animal, the Swallow asked:

"Well, Wasp. Were you successful today? Did you find out which animal's meat tastes the best?"

The Wasp answered: "Indeed I did, Swallow! After tasting hundreds of different animals, I found that the human beings are the most delicious of all. From now on, our respected Khan-Garid must eat only humans."

The Wasp's surprising announcement greatly upset the Swallow, as he liked the men and women of the Earth.

"Oh dear," thought the Swallow. "How can I save those poor Humans from being hunted by Khan-Garid for eternity?"

Devising a plan, the Swallow asked the Wasp: "Brother, how did you manage to taste the Humans?"

"Oh! It was easy," replied the Wasp. "I pierced their skins with my stinger and tasted their blood with my tongue!"

"How interesting!" exclaimed the Swallow. " Where is this powerful tongue of yours?"

And when the Wasp opened its mouth to show the bird its tongue, as quick as quick can be, the Swallow pecked it out.

Before the shocked Wasp could react, the two flying creatures were called before the Khan-Garid.

"So, tell me what you have discovered," boomed the Khan. "Wasp, you speak first!"

But the tongueless Wasp could no longer speak. All it could do was fly round and round the great Khan's head, protesting and complaining with a loud buzzing sound.

"What in Heaven's name are you trying to say, Wasp?" roared the Khan. "I can't understand a single word!"

In exasperation, Khan-Garid shooed away the droning Wasp.

"Swallow," he said. "You tell me whose meat is the sweetest."

"With pleasure, Your Majesty," replied the Swallow. "The tastiest meat in the world belongs to the snake."

Thanking the Swallow, Khan-Garid vowed to hunt and eat only snakes from that day on. This royal tradition is still carried on today by the descendant of Khan-Garid, the eagle.

As for the Wasp, from the moment the Swallow pecked out its tongue it lost its voice completely and now it can only make a whining, buzzing sound. If you've ever felt a Wasp's sting, you are also aware that losing its tongue did not make the Wasp any kinder.

Khan-Garid: the Mongolian name for the Garuda, a mythological bird from India. A bird of great power, the Garuda's wings are so large that when it flies its wings screen the sun and the moon. In 1994 the Garuda was adopted as the official bird of the Mongolian capital, Ulaanbaatar.

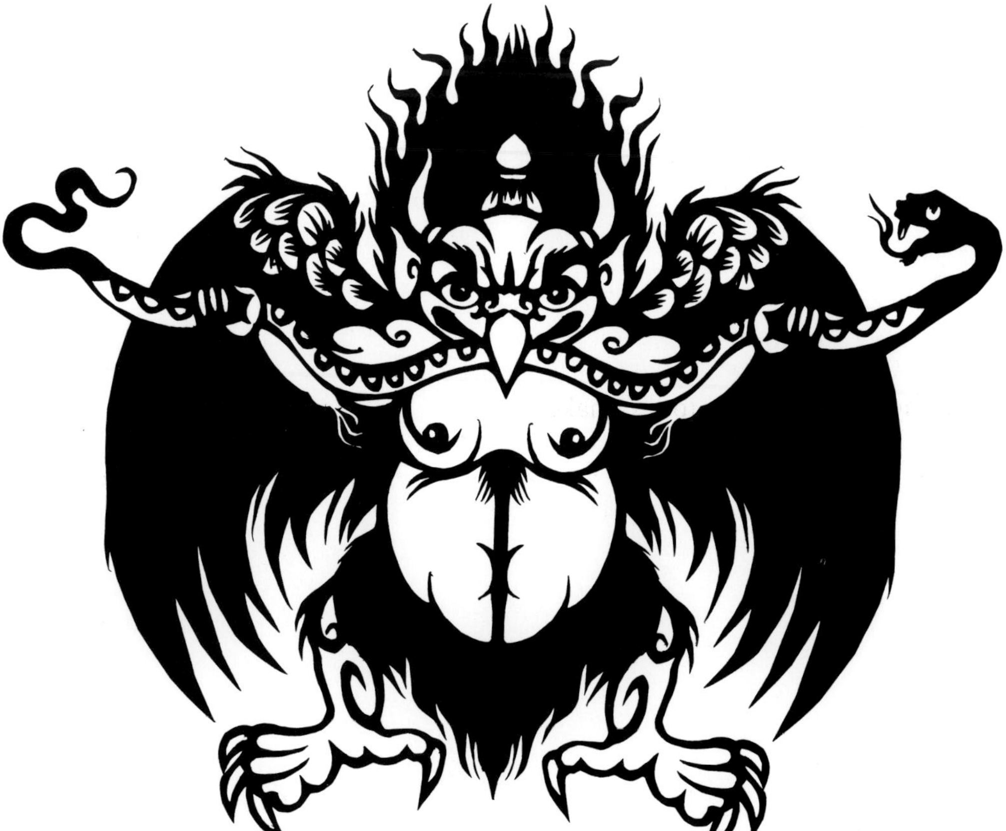

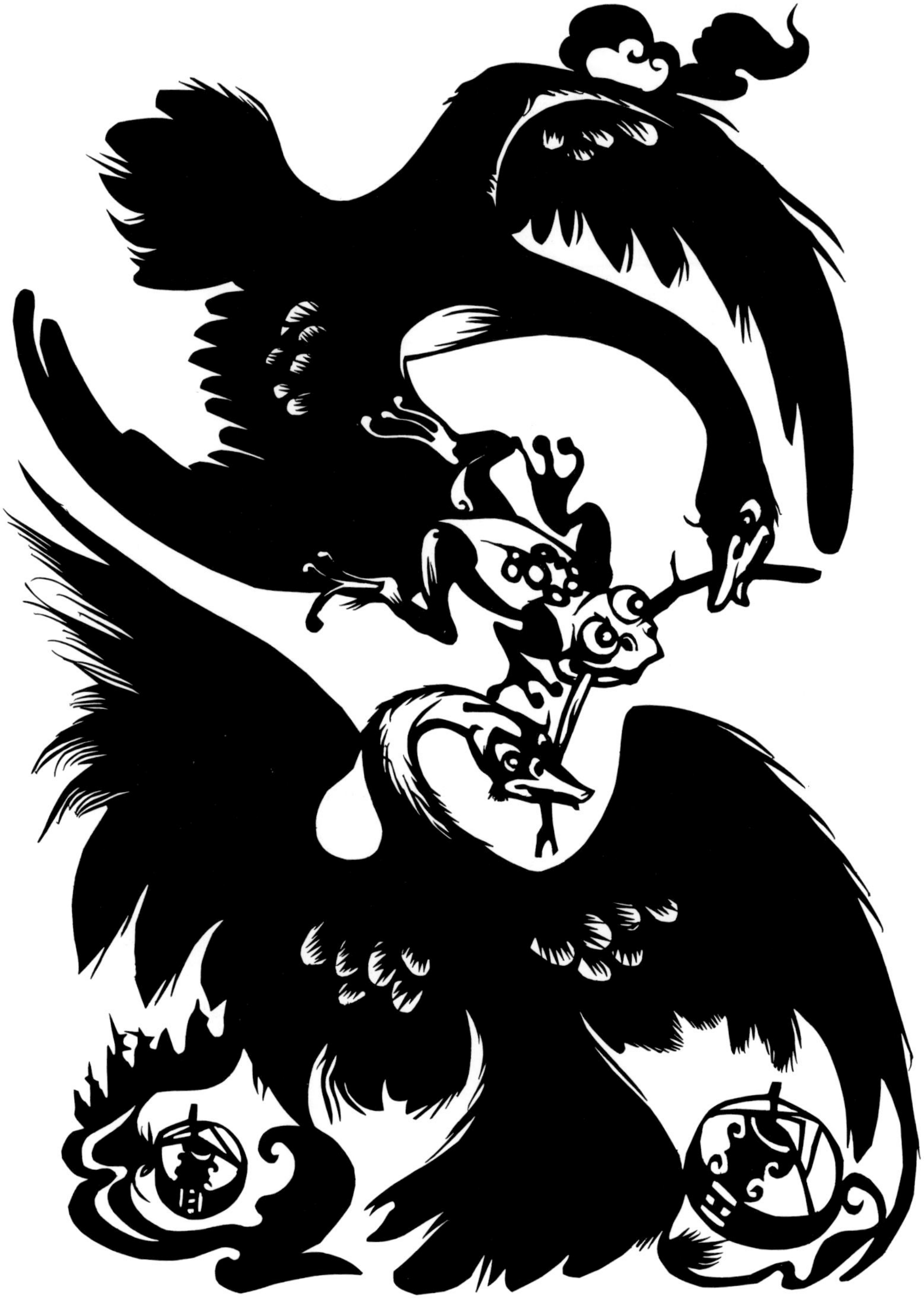

The flying frog

On the edge of beautiful Lake Hovsgol in the north of Mongolia lived a flock of geese and one small frog. As autumn approached and the world grew cool, the geese began to discuss plans to fly south for the winter.

The frog overheard the geese talking about the warmth and joys of southern climes, and felt sorry for himself. Shaking his head sadly, he said to the geese with bitterness:

"Oh! What a life has a little earthbound frog! I am destined to spend all my days wallowing in this cold mud! But you! How happy you geese must be to fly across the big sky, to see the world beneath you, and feel the warm sun on your backs in winter!"

The head goose felt sorry for the little frog. Winter in Mongolia was indeed brutally cold. Turning to his flock, he said:

"Brothers, we geese have wings and the frog doesn't. But we are all one family in the animal world. Let's help the frog and show him something of this wonderful world. Who can think of a way to carry the frog with us as we fly south?"

The geese consulted each other. Finally one goose picked up a willow twig and suggested:

"What about this? While the frog bites down firmly on the middle of this branch, two of us can clamp the ends in our beaks. This way we can carry the frog as we fly through the sky."

The head goose agreed to this clever idea and chose two of the biggest and strongest geese to transport the frog.

When the time came to leave , the delighted frog opened his mouth and bit firmly onto the willow branch. Off he flew, high in the sky with the flock of geese, saying goodbye to his muddy home. Looking down on the world from a great height, the frog thought to himself:

"How wonderful this is! Even though I don't have wings, I am flying at the head of these migrating geese. How clever I am!"

For many hours the geese flew effortlessly southwards while the little frog hung on and marvelled at the changing sights below. As more time passed, with the refreshing wind in his face and the sun warming his back, the self-satisfied frog grew more and more confident and felt himself to be more and more powerful.

When the flock flew over an encampment of several *gers,* the people herding sheep and goats below looked up, pointed, and exclaimed:

"Look at that! Look at those geese! Two of them are carrying a frog on a branch. What clever geese they are!"

The people were very impressed by the intelligence of the geese and marvelled at the incredible sight until the big birds had faded out of sight. But the flying frog had heard the people's shouts of wonder and became rather irritated and jealous. He said to himself:

"Why are these geese being praised? I'm the one that's flying through the air!"

And the frog began to become resentful of the geese.

Later in the afternoon, the geese flew over a small lake. The mud-bound frogs below looked up and stared in amazement. Enviously, they all began croaking at the geese, saying,

"Hey! What about us! We want to fly too!"

The flying frog observed his cousins in the mud below with disdain and thought:

"Ha! you poor devils! I'm the only frog that knows how to fly!"

And he opened his boastful mouth to tell them as much:

"Hey, cousins, look at me! Flying's a breeze when you're clever as I am!"

You can imagine what happened next. The moment he opened his big, bragging mouth, the flying frog slipped off the willow branch carried by the two powerful geese and dropped to his death on the cold, damp earth.

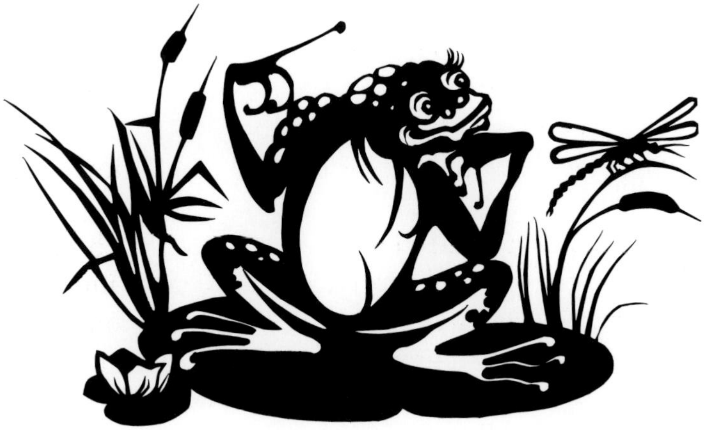

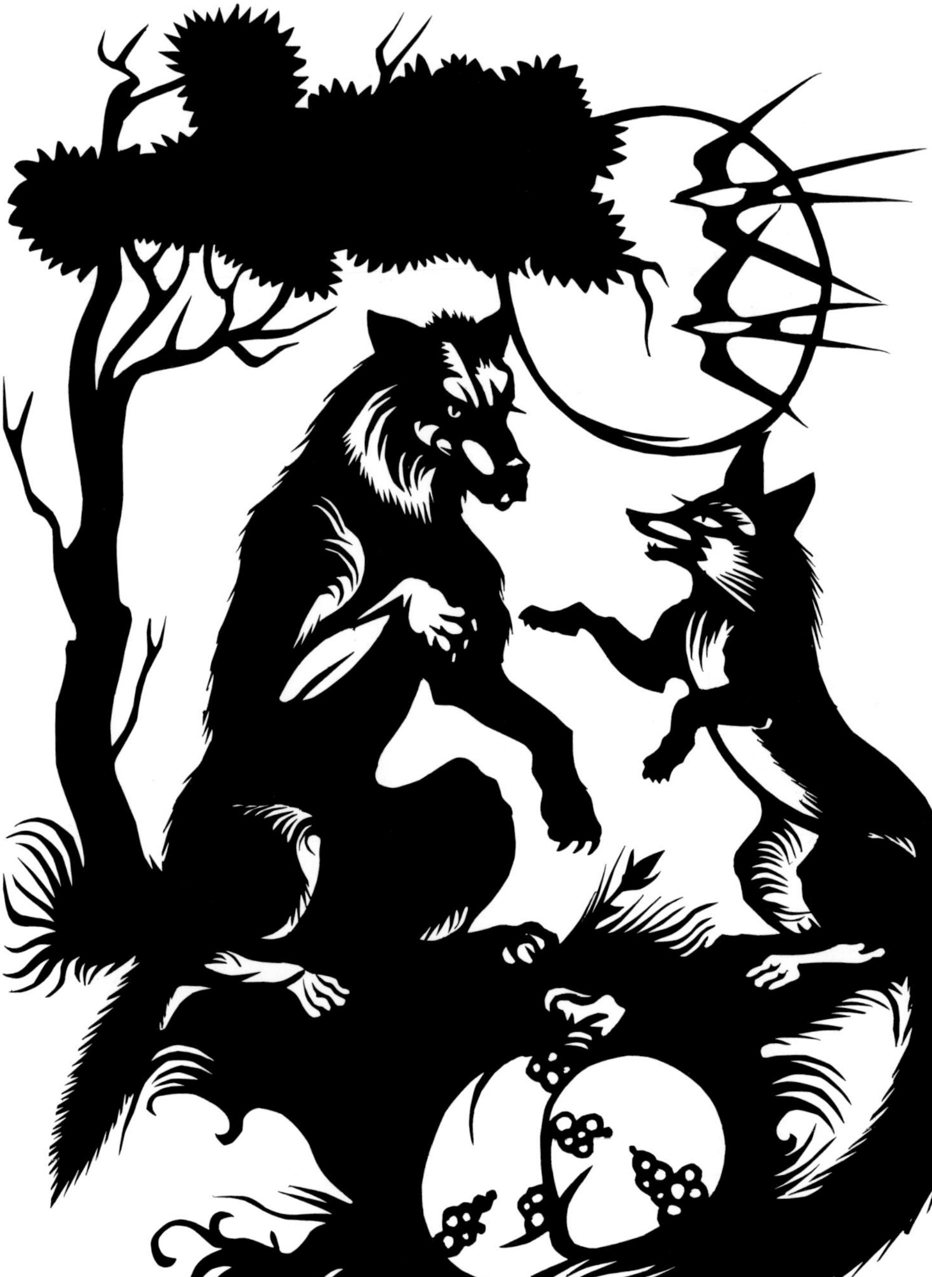

THE FOX, THE WOLF AND THE BAG OF BUTTER

One day, as a she-Fox and a he-Wolf were hunting together, they came upon a bag full of butter that some human had accidentally dropped by the side of the road.

The two animals agreed to divide the butter equally between them, but suddenly the Fox said:

"It's not a good idea to eat the butter here by the roadside. Someone might come along and disturb us. Let's take the bag up to the mountaintop and eat it there."

So the two animals carried the butter to the top of a high mountain. Just as the Wolf prepared to start eating his share, the Fox said:

"It's not a good idea to share this butter. Only one of us should eat it."

The Wolf asked: "Well then, which of us should get to eat it?"

"The one of us who is oldest," answered the Fox. "How old are you?"

The Wolf, who wanted that butter all to himself very much, decided to try and trick the Fox. He said to her:

"When I was little the Great Mountain Sumber was just a small mound of earth, and the Big Lake Hovsgol was a tiny puddle."

On hearing this the Fox burst into tears. The Wolf, surprised, thought to himself:

"Oh, poor sensitive Fox! But it doesn't matter to me whether you cry or not because now the bag of butter will all be mine!"

Still, curious to know why the Fox was so stricken with grief, the Wolf asked her, "Why are you so sad?"

Whereupon the Fox, wiping her tears, said in a choked voice:

"I have three cubs. My youngest is exactly the same age as you. When you mentioned your childhood, I began to think of my youngest cub and I miss him so much that I began to cry!"

Her story saddened the Wolf and suddenly he was ashamed of himself for his trickery. He gave the bag of butter to the Fox and went slinking off to his lair, his mouth still watering over the lost delicacy.

When the Wolf was out of sight, the sly Fox began to eat the butter all by herself, chuckling between each delicious mouthful.

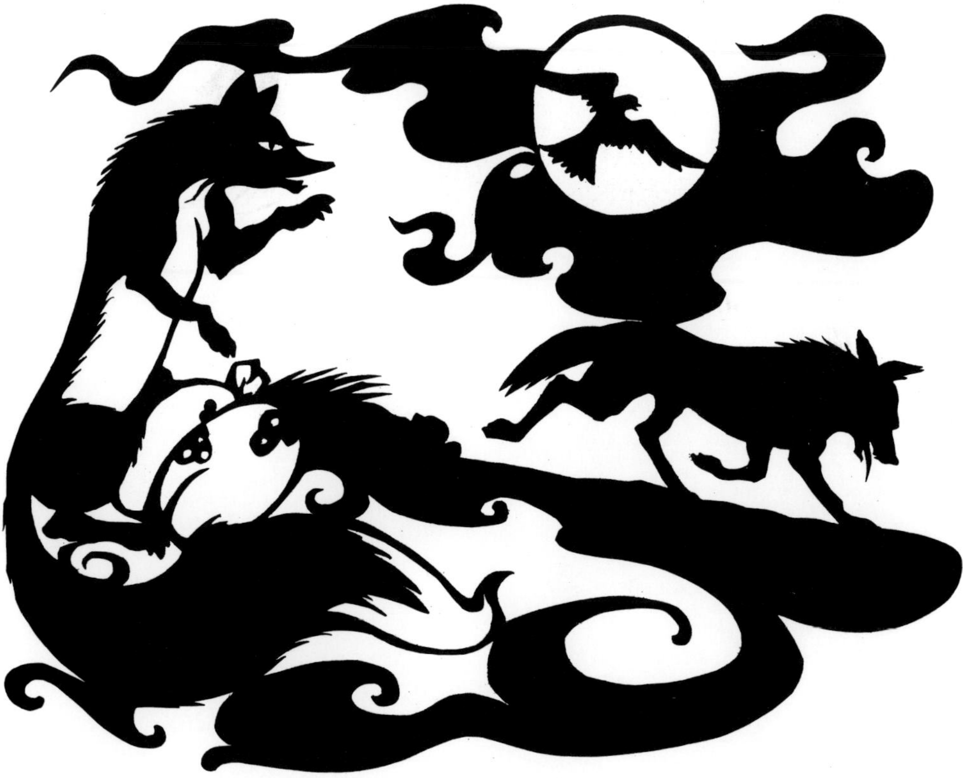

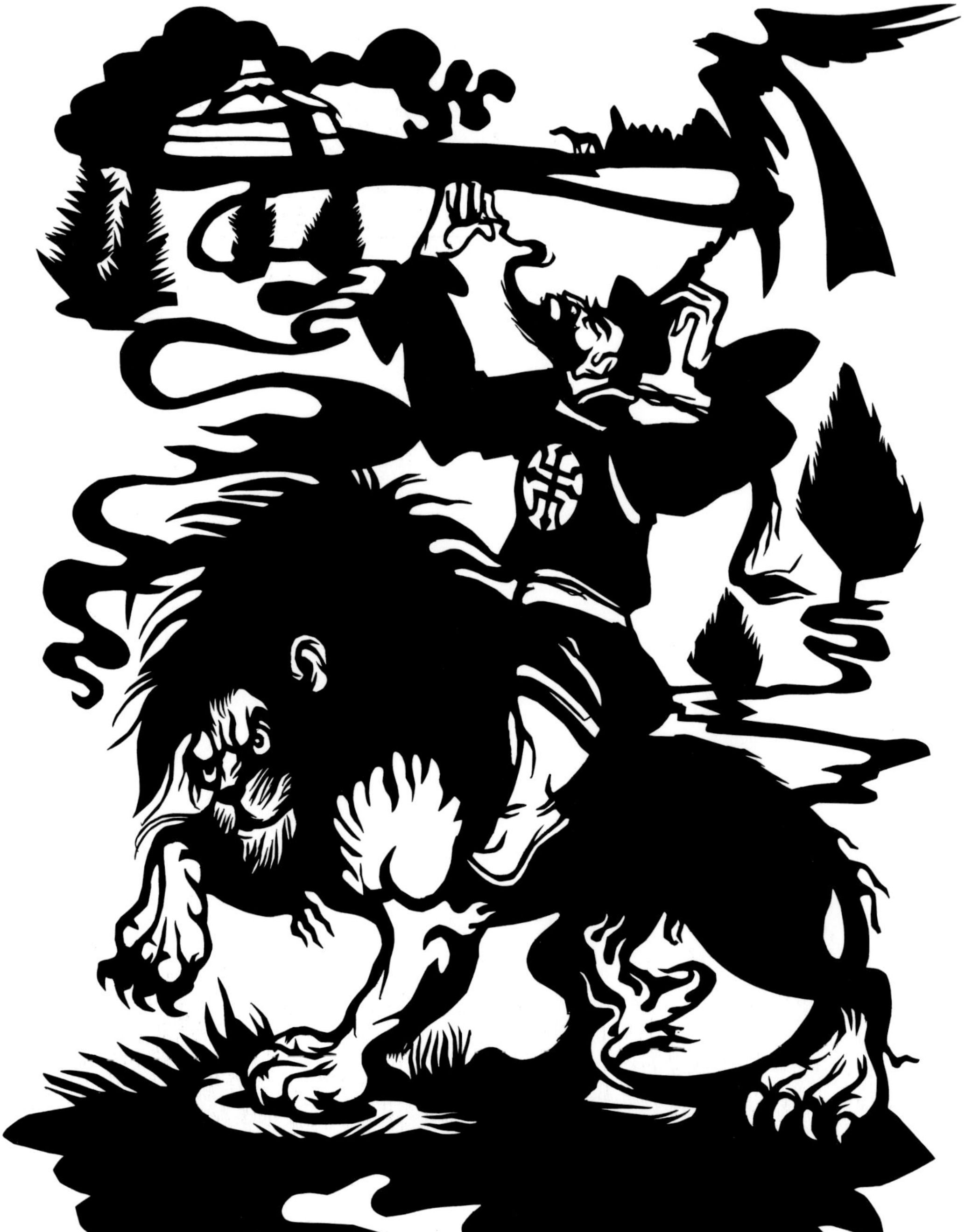

The Old Man and the Lion

There once lived an old couple near the Selenge forest of Mongolia. One morning the old man got up earlier than usual and went outside to check his few thin horses. As he stepped out of his *ger*, he suddenly saw a hungry-looking young lion coming towards him. Frightened by the ferocious-looking animal, the old man ducked back in the *ger* and locked the small door tight. Shaking his still-sleeping wife, he cried:

"Old woman, wake up! There's a big lion outside! It's coming to get us! Whatever shall we do?"

The wife, rubbing sleep from her eyes, told her trembling husband between yawns:

"Listen, old man. The one with the most power doesn't necessarily win. The one who is more clever can be the winner sometimes too. Take your *urga** and go directly up to the lion. The Lion will ask where you're going. Tell him you're going to catch a lion for dinner. Then…"

And the wife continued telling her husband what he should do. When she had finished, the old man smiled and did as his wife had advised. He went out of the *ger* and met the lion, who growled:

"Hey, old man! Where are you going?"

"Why, I'm off to catch a lion for our dinner, but it looks like I won't have to go far!"

"What?" said the lion, very surprised. "How can an old man like you catch a strong lion like me? I'm a hundred times more powerful than you are. Ha! I could kill you with one swipe of my paw!"

Laughing loudly, the old man replied:

"Oh, you can, can you? Well, let's just see about that. Let's have a contest to see which of us is the stronger. If you're more powerful than I am, you can kill me. If I'm the stronger, you'll become my slave."

The lion agreed, knowing that he would have no trouble winning any contest with such a feeble old man.

The two contestants went out onto the open steppe to begin the test. There the old man picked up a small round stone and showed it to the lion.

"Squeeze this stone in your paws until its juice runs out. If you can do this, you'll be the winner."

The powerful lion squeezed the stone with all his might, but not one drop of juice came out.

Then the old man took a goose egg out of his pocket and said:

"Now it's my turn. Watch and see how powerful I am!"

Squeezing the egg in just one hand, the old man crushed the shell, sending its liquid spurting to the ground.

Showing the crushed egg to the lion, the old man told him:

"You see! The stone is completely destroyed! So, who do you think is the most powerful?"

The lion, astounded, admitted defeat and let himself become the old man's slave. The old man pierced the lion's nose and led it around by a rope; then he haltered the lion and rode him like a horse.

For a whole week the old man ordered the lion to do all the heavy work around the *ger* and proudly rode the tamed animal over the steppe. The lion was completely humiliated.

At the end of the first hard week, the old man ordered the lion to go into the forest so that the old man could find willows to make a bow and some arrows. Tied to a tree, the lion waited patiently, observing how the old man tried with great effort and little succcss to break off the thin branches of a willow. Slowly the lion became suspicious of the old man's strength as he watched him sweat and heave to get the branch. On the journey home, the lion turned to the old man and asked him:

"Old man, what happened to your power? Back there in the forest you couldn't even tear off a willow branch. I'm beginning to think that you must have tricked me!"

The old man said nothing, but the moment he got home he ran in a panic to his wife.

"Old woman," he cried. "The lion has discovered how weak I am! Now he'll kill me for sure!"

"Stop worrying, you silly old man," said the wife. "Tomorrow, when the lion returns, you ask me loudly, 'What are you going to prepare for my supper, old woman?' You'll see what will happen."

The next day the old man did as instructed. When the lion approached the *ger*, the old man shouted to his wife:

"Old woman! What are you going to cook tonight for my supper?"

"Don't be so impatient" shouted back the old woman. "Will you be satisfied if I boil up pieces of last week's old lion with the fresh meat of a young lion's shank?"

Upon overhearing this, the lion thought to himself,

"What do my ears hear? These old people are planning to kill me and eat me! I'd better run away while I'm still alive!"

And the lion ran off to the safety of the forest as fast as he could. On the way, he met a fox who asked him:

"Lion, where are you off to in such a hurry? And what has happened to you? You have a stick through your nose, just like a camel!"

The lion explained everything that had happened over the past week. When he had finished his story, the fox began to laugh:

"Why, Lion," he said. "How stupid you've been. That clever old man has really tricked you. No man has ever had such power! Let's go together and kill those old people. You attack the old man first, then catch the old woman. But don't forget to share the prey with me!"

Together the two animals ran back to the old couple's *ger* by the edge of the forest. When the old man, who was tending his horses, saw them coming, he ran to his wife to tell her that this time they were doomed for sure.

As the lion and the fox approached the *ger*, the old woman stepped out, alone. Looking squarely at the fox and shaking the finger of one hand, she shouted angrily:

"Why, you lazy, sly old fox! You promised to bring me a nice fat lion for dinner tonight. What makes you think you can come with this skinny thing!"

The lion was stunned. Him? The old couple's dinner? Turning on the smaller animal whom he believed had tricked him, the lion roared, "Why you trickster!" and slaughtered the fox at once.

As the lion bounded off to the forest once and for all, the old couple fell into each other's arms and laughed until the tears streamed down their wrinkled cheeks. It is because of this terrible experience with Man that, to this very day, the lion keeps well clear of the *gers* of the Mongols.

And the lion probably doesn't trust the fox much anymore, either.

**Urga: the Mongolian horse-catching pole.*

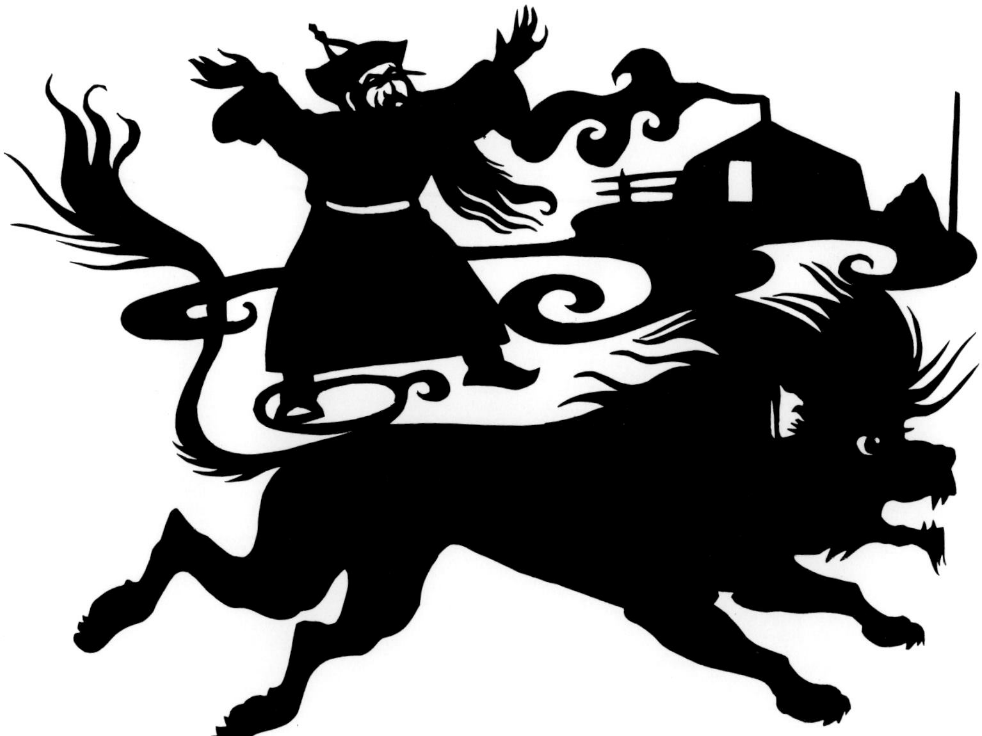

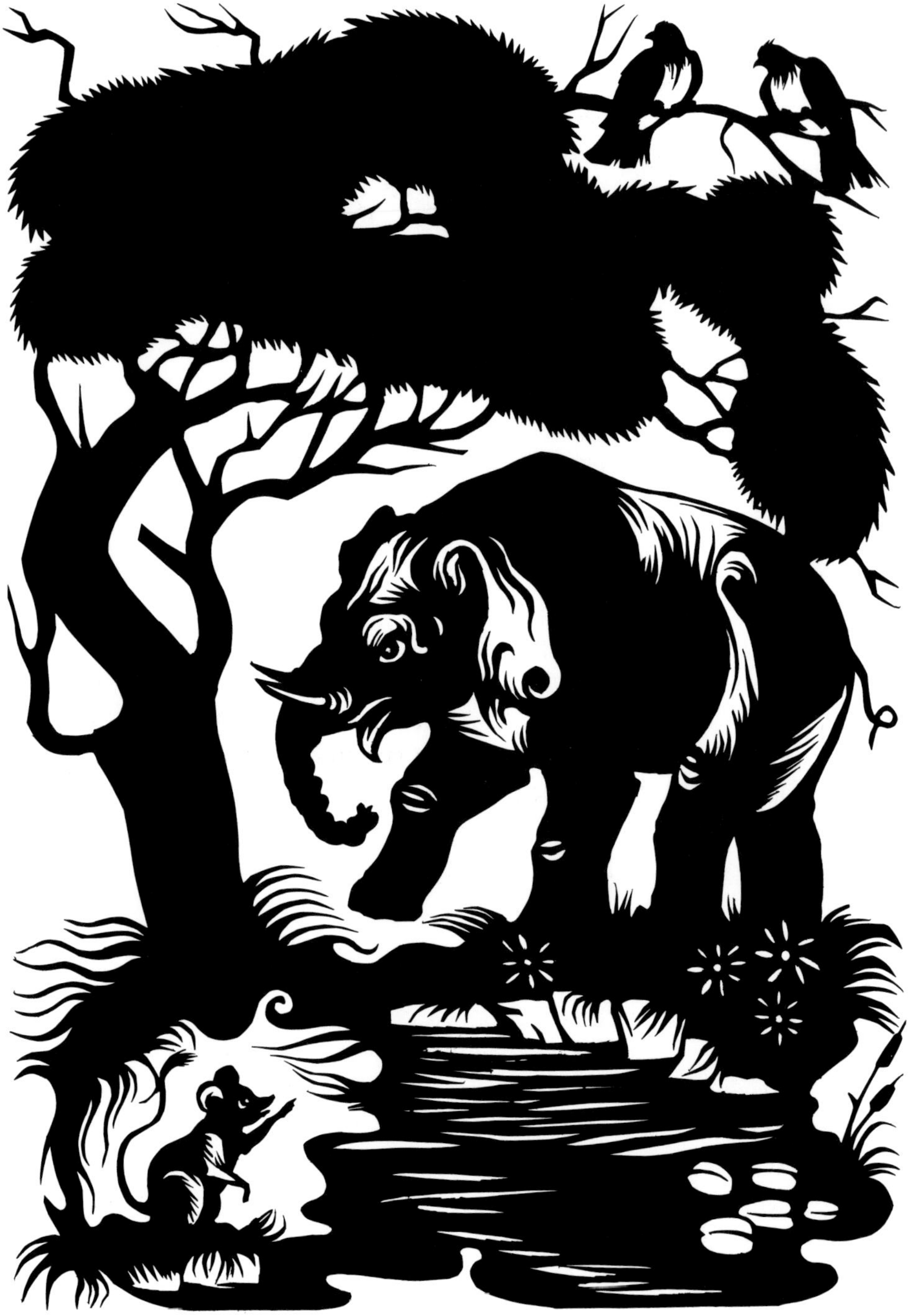

The Mouse Who Battled the Elephant

Not too long ago, there was a Mouse who made its home in the bank of a wide, peaceful river.

Every few days, a large, mean-spirited Elephant would come to the river to bathe and drink. When the Elephant had finished washing and quenching its thirst, it would always play the same cruel trick on the defenceless Mouse, a joke that the Elephant thought was very funny. Using his long trunk like a hose, the Elephant would squirt water deep into the Mouse's hole, completely washing away its little home. This went on for a long time.

You can imagine how the Mouse suffered from this nasty trick. For months the Mouse tried for months to get the Elephant to stop, begging the big animal to cease its pointless destruction. Each time, the Elephant would just laugh, ignoring the little Mouse's desperate pleas.

Finally, the Mouse decided, "Enough!" The next time the Elephant came to wash, the Mouse stood as high as he possibly could on a rock and, shaking a little finger, squeaked:

"Elephant. I'm warning you! If you ruin my house one more time, I will declare war on you! And I tell you now: you will be very sorry indeed!"

The pachyderm, who could crush the Mouse with one of its huge feet, trumpeted with laughter on hearing these threats from such a tiny creature.

"You? Battle me? Ha! Ha! Ha!"

Drawing water up his long trunk, the Elephant once again flooded the little animal's hole. Then, swinging his trunk back and forth uproariously, off he tromped, his leathery hide shaking with each deep chuckle.

Watching the big gray bully disappear down the bank, the Mouse, tears of anger and frustration brimming in his eyes, clenched his sharp little teeth and began planning his Revenge.

A few days later the Elephant came to the river at his regular bath hour. But this time, when he lowered his long nose in the stream to draw water for his nasty trick, the tiny rodent scurried up inside his trunk. Working itself deep into the brute's body, the Mouse began the counterattack: it scratched at the Elephant's lungs, bit his heart, gnawed his kidneys and his liver, then wriggled its tiny body up and down the Elephant's intestines, wreaking terrible damage wherever it turned.

The horrified Elephant roared with shock and pain. Trying desperately to dislodge the Mouse, the dying Elephant ranted and raved and rolled and rammed into everything in sight. The battle raged just minutes but the path of destruction stretched as far as the eye could see: the earth was laid flat, whole trees and bushes were torn from their roots, large boulders were thrown asunder. The countryside looked like a battlefield, and all this because of a little Mouse.

When the dust settled, the Mouse, avenged for all its suffering, emerged triumphantly from the trunk of the lifeless beast and hurried back to its now undisturbed hole in the riverbank.

Living peacefully and happily for many years after, the Mouse often told this story to his children, his many grandchildren, and later to his many, many great-grandchildren. And the story would always end with these words:

"Little ones, you must always remember that Might does not mean Right. And no matter what size the adversary, we little creatures, when wronged, can always find a way to defend ourselves."

They certainly did, the time the Mouse battled the Elephant.

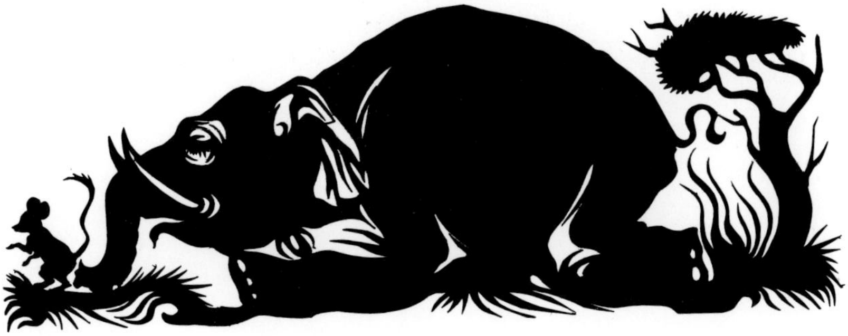

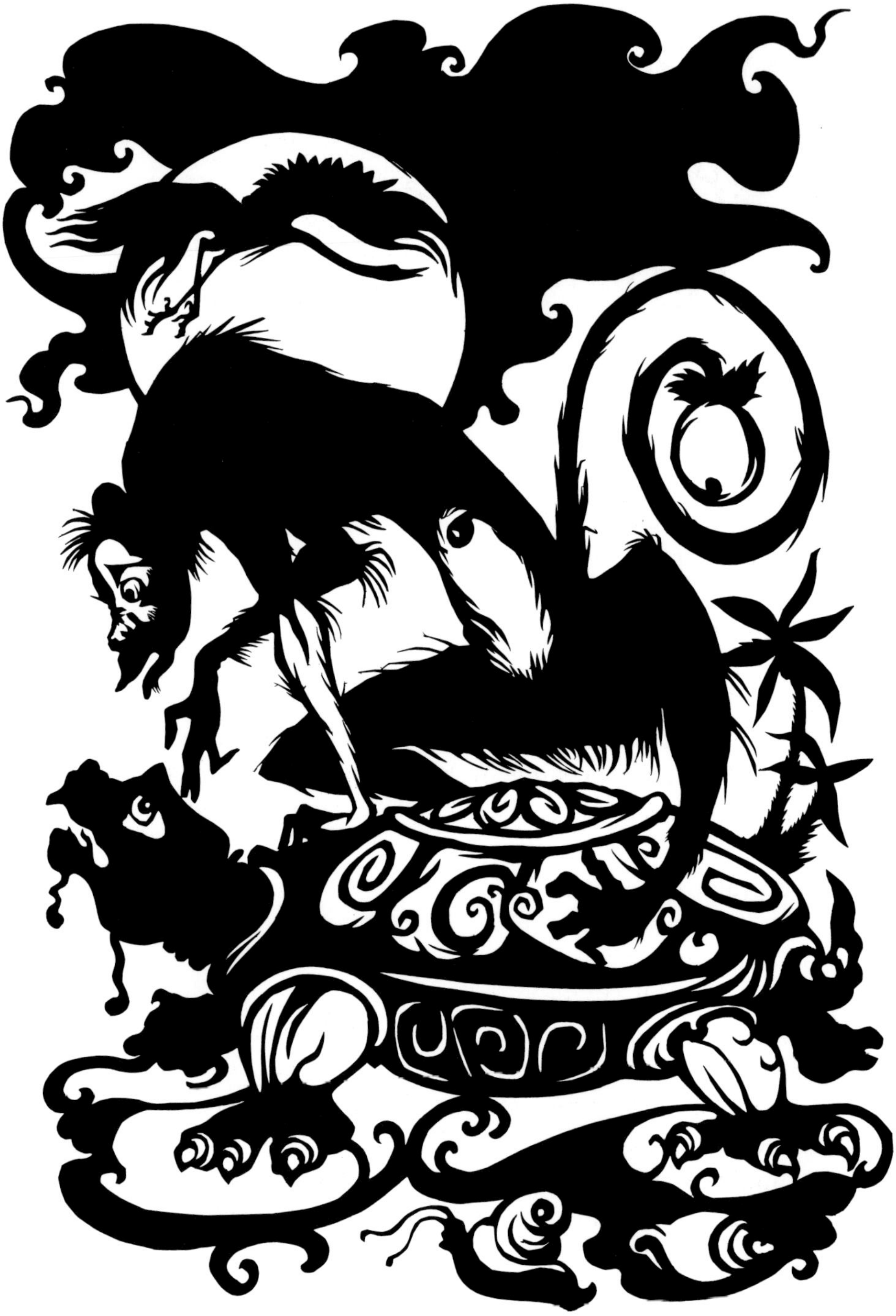

The Turtle and the Monkey

Did you know that there are he-turtles and she-turtles, and that she-turtles can be very suspicious and jealous? This is a story of what happened one day, a long time ago.

A he-turtle went up to the mountains on business one afternoon, and there he met a monkey. They introduced themselves to each other, became friendly, and had long conversations about this and that. When the he-turtle finished his business the next day he returned home feeling very satisfied with his trip and his new female friend. The he-turtle's she-turtle became suspicious of the cheerful smile on her husband's face and said to herself:

"Hmm. It looks as though my he-turtle had a fine old time up in the mountains. He probably met one of those cute she-monkeys!"

In her jealousy the she-turtle devised a plan to punish her husband. The next morning she stayed in bed, moaning:

"Oh! I feel so sick today!"

The concerned he-turtle asked:

"Whatever is the matter, my dear? And what will help you recover?"

"The only thing that will help me," groaned the she-turtle, "is the heart of a she-monkey. I must eat a she-monkey's heart or I shall surely die!"

The he-turtle, alarmed at his wife's terrible condition, hurried back to the mountains and called out for his friend, the only she-monkey he knew. When he found her he told her, not altogether truthfully:

"We became such good friends a few days ago that I thought I should invite you to my home and prepare a nice dinner for you."

The she-monkey, greatly flattered, accepted the invitation and the two set out together, chatting all the way.

Soon they arrived at the he-turtle's house. Before going inside he turned to the she-monkey and said:

"My wife is unwell. The only thing that will help her recover is a she-monkey's heart. I would like to take your heart out to heal my wife."

The quick-witted she-monkey exclaimed:

"But turtle, why didn't you tell me about this when we were at my house? Don't you know that monkeys hang their hearts from the treetops! We must quickly return together to my house and fetch my heart for your sick wife!"

So the two animals set out again for the mountains. The he-turtle waited patiently at the bottom of the she-monkey's tree while the monkey climbed way up to the top. Once up as high as she could go, she took some of her droppings and threw them down at the he-turtle, shouting:

"What a nice friend you turned out to be! Let your 'sick' wife eat this, my 'heart.'"

The monkey stayed up in her tree laughing, while the turtle plodded home to his wife.

He was all alone…and smelling not a little unpleasantly.

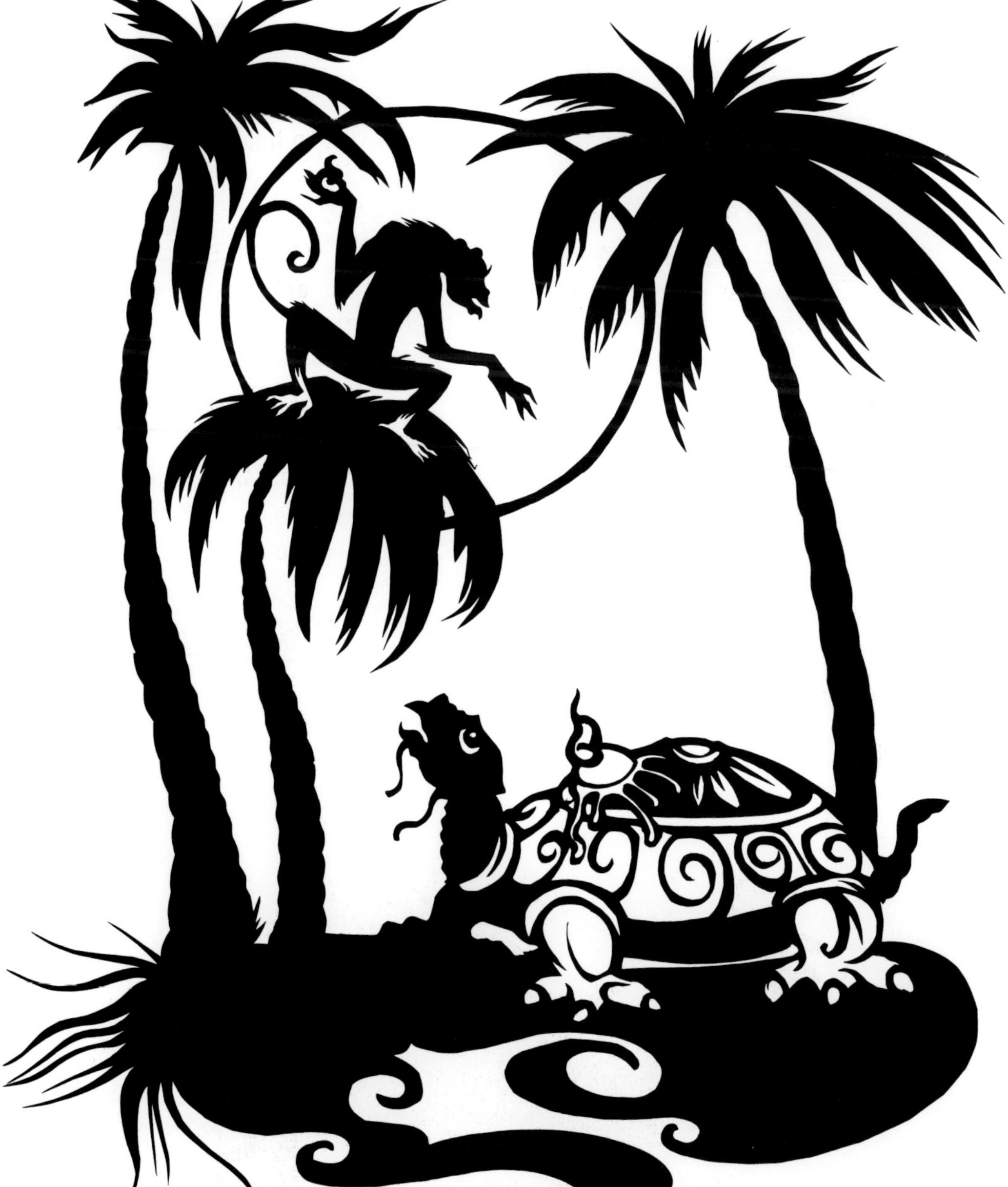

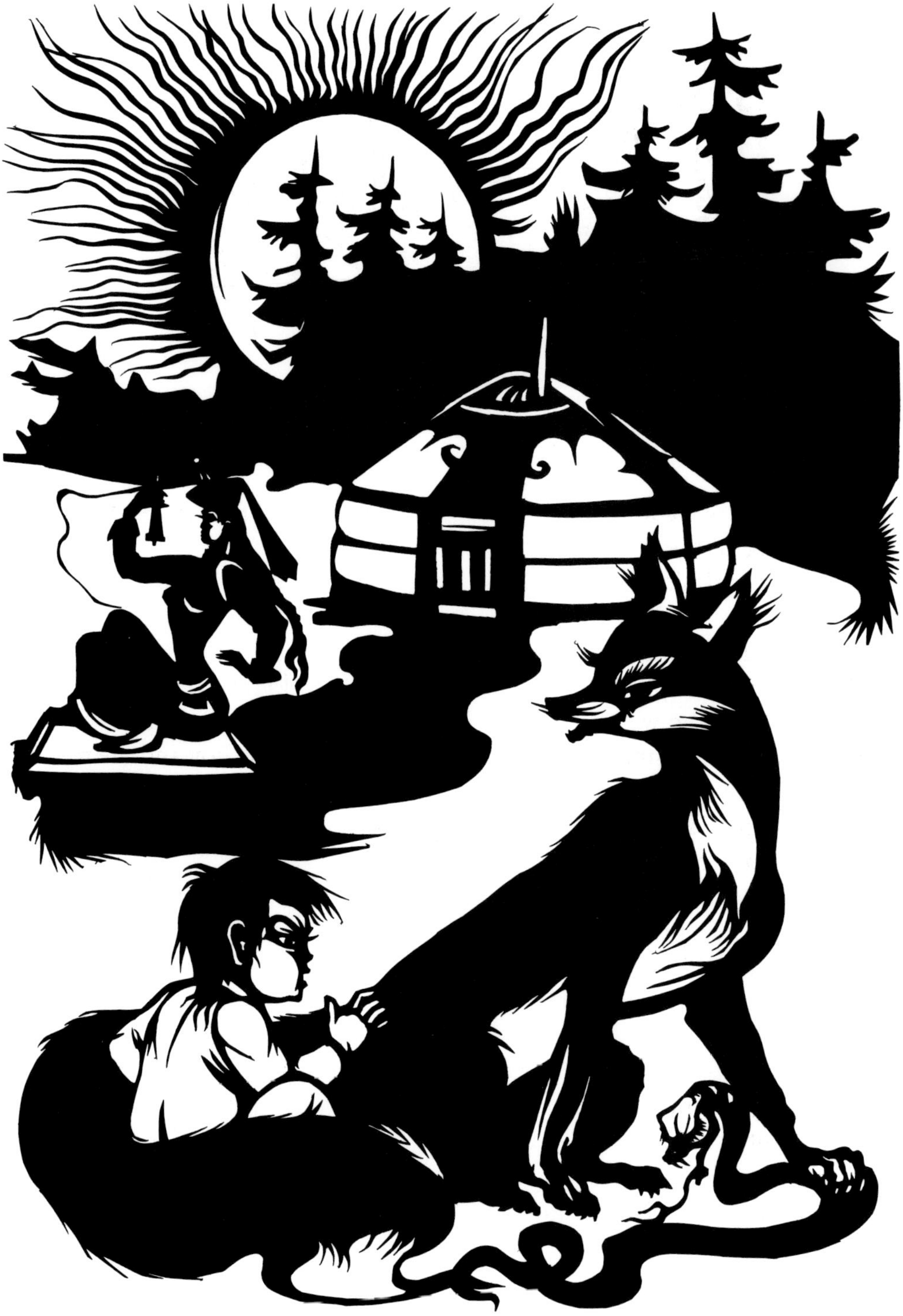

The Faithful Little Fox

Here is a story about why we should never do anything without first getting all the facts.

A hunter and his wife once lived happily with their small son near the vast, silent forests of Mongolia. One day, the hunter caught a baby fox and brought it home to his child as a pet and playmate.

The little fox was playful and mischievous and soon became a great friend to the little boy, who was fond of it. While the father went hunting and the mother tended their small herds, she would often leave the boy and the fox together to play. When she returned home, the little fox would run merrily to greet her, jump about and turn somersaults, which always made her laugh.

Many happy months passed.

One day, when the mother returned from helping her husband in the forest, she was surprised that the little fox did not run to meet her as it always had. Instead, the fox sat near the threshold of the *ger*, whining pitifully. When the mother came closer, she saw that the animal was covered with blood.

"Oh no! Oh heavens!" she cried. "The fox has ripped my child to shreds!"

Grabbing a stone, she struck the little fox till it was dead and then burst screaming into the *ger*.

There she saw her little son, as fat and happy as ever, clapping his hands and laughing merrily. Next to him lay a large, dead snake that had been torn to pieces.

She wept, wringing her hands in sadness. "What a terrible thing I have done!" she said. And she swore at herself for being hasty and wrongly judging the faithful little fox.

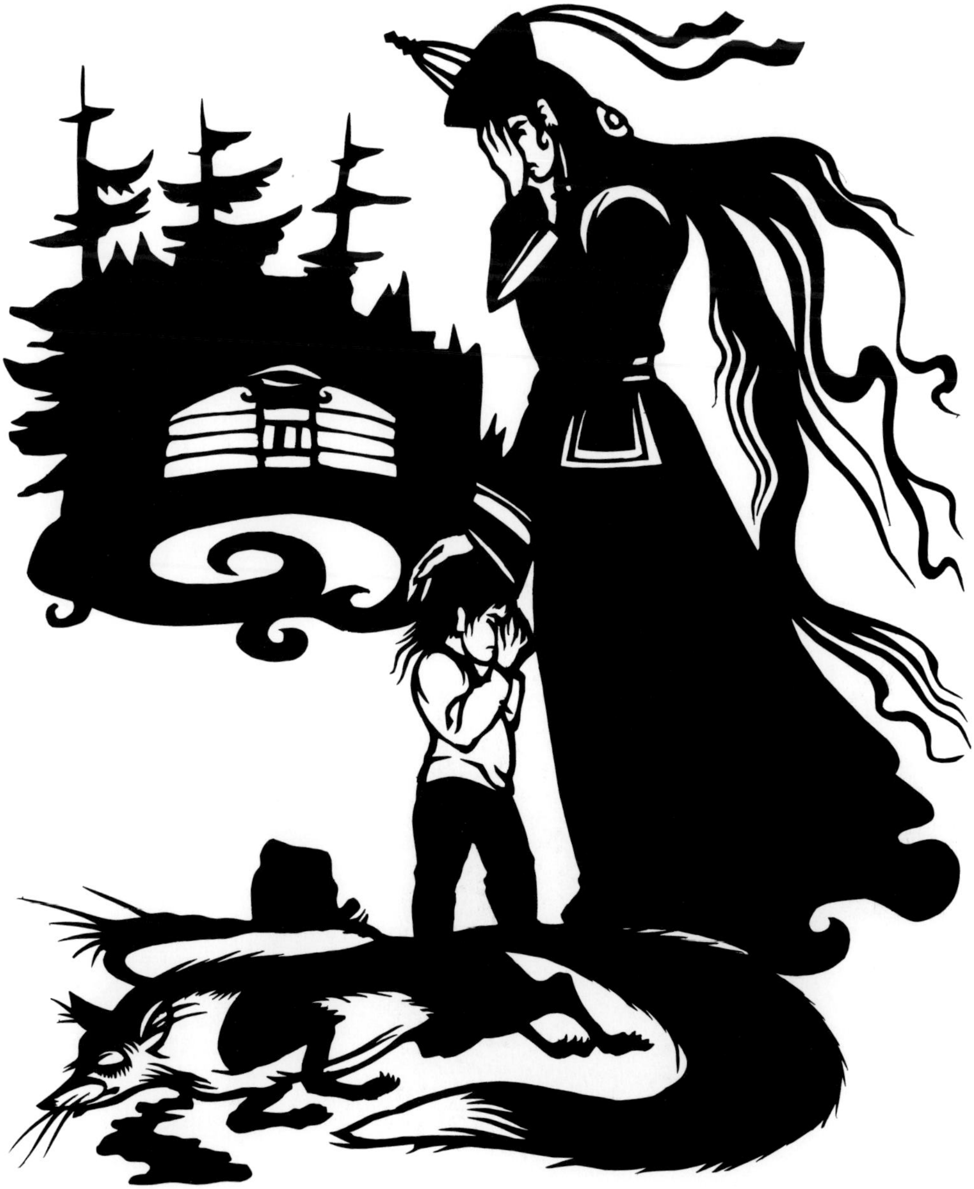

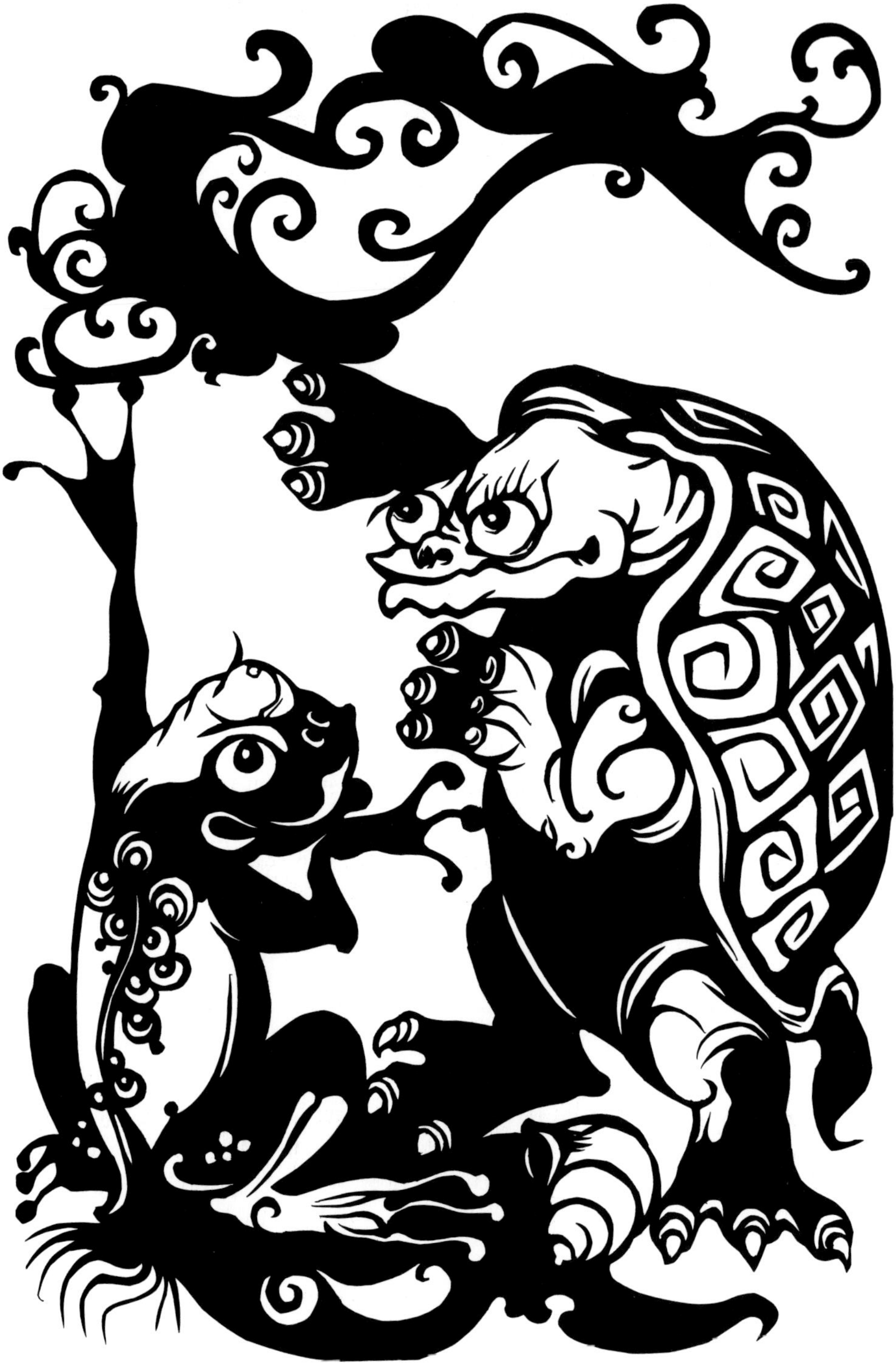

The Tale of the One-Eyed Frog and the Turtle

Once upon a time, in the northwest corner of Mongolia, there lived a Frog who had only one good eye with which to see. The Frog had been born in a small well, and had spent his whole uneventful life there. Indeed, the well was the Frog's entire world.

One night a great storm broke out, sending torrents of rain over the land. The wind blew harder and harder and the waves of Uvs Nur, the largest Mongolian sea, rose higher and higher. In the chaos of the unrelenting downpour, a little sea turtle was suddenly thrown out of the roiling waters onto the land.

When the storm abated the next day and the sun came out at last, the Turtle opened its eyes and found itself in an unfamiliar place. It looked about in every possible direction, but could see the Uvs Nur Sea nowhere. Determined to find its vast watery home again, the Turtle set out on its quest but gradually became more and more lost and hungry and thirsty.

For days, the poor desperate Turtle wandered, until at last it reached the brink of Death itself.

Just as the Turtle was taking its final steps, it stumbled upon the well where the Frog lived. The Frog was most surprised to see another living thing and questioned the Turtle:

"Who are you? What are you? Where did you come from? Where are you going?"

The Turtle, revived after eating a bit of moss and drinking a sip of water, told the Frog:

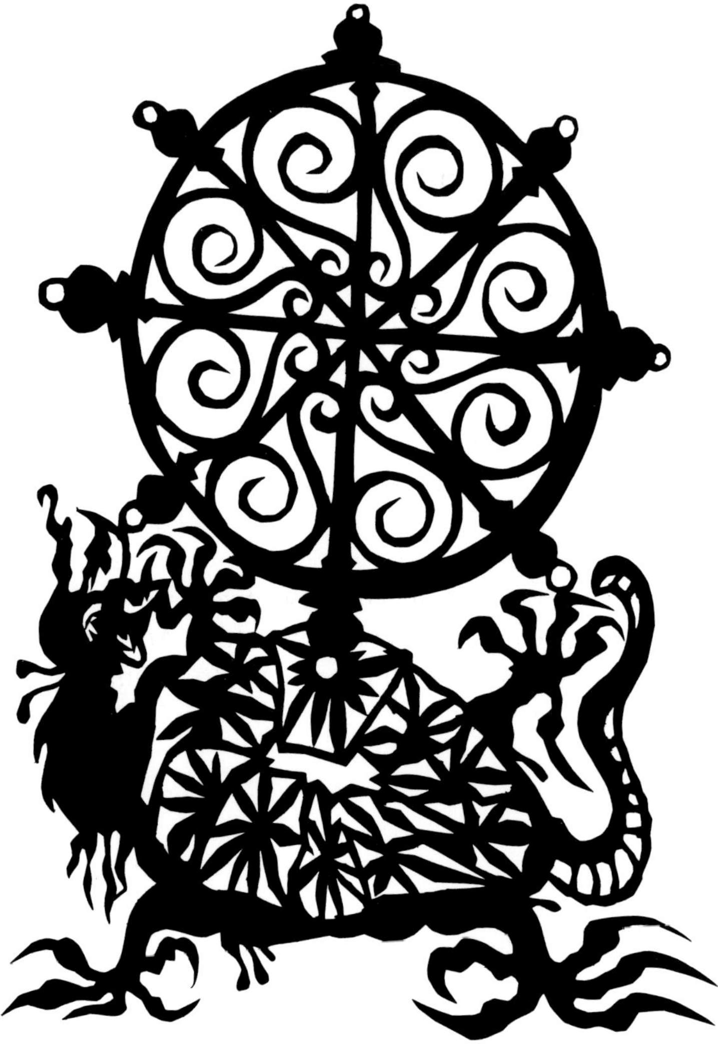

"I am a Turtle. I live in the great Uvs Nur Sea. Not long ago there was a violent storm and I was thrown up by the waves onto the land. I lost my way trying to find my home. Instead, I have found you."

The Frog said: "What are you going to do now?"

The Turtle replied: "I want to return to my home, the great Sea, but it is very far away and I don't know in which direction to travel. I shall surely die if I leave here, so I suppose I must stay. Could I live here with you in your well as your neighbor?"

Then the Frog, showing the Turtle one-third of its well water, asked the newcomer:

"Is your 'Sea' water about this size?"

"Oh no!" the Turtle replied. "The Uvs Nur Sea is much greater than that!"

The Frog, showing the Turtle two-thirds of its well, asked the Turtle:

"What about this size, then? Is your 'Sea' about like this?"

To which the Turtle replied, "Mr. Frog, it is impossible to compare my Sea to this small well! The Uvs Nur is so big that it cannot be measured."

Hearing this statement, which it thought impossible and absurd, the one-eyed Frog became angry and began shouting at the Turtle, saying:

"What are you talking about! This 'Sea' of yours, even if it is big, cannot possibly be bigger than my well! I know everything. And you are just a tramp and a beggar who is praising your own home, this thing you call a 'Sea,' to try and impress me. 'Measureless Sea,' indeed! Be off with you, you liar!"

And the blind-eyed Frog drove the poor lost Turtle away from its well.

The Turtle, in disbelief at the Frog's simple-mindedness, looked it straight in its one good eye and said slowly and clearly:

"All right, Frog. You are free to think what you want to think, but you really are a stupid creature. You may have one good eye, but your mind is completely blind. Your knowledge is restricted to the boundaries of this tiny well. There are many who know a great deal more about life and the world than you do: you should listen to them and learn from their experience!"

With that the Turtle turned on its heel and left. Eventually it found the great Uvs Nur Sea, which was not in fact too far away, and plunged happily back into its coolness.

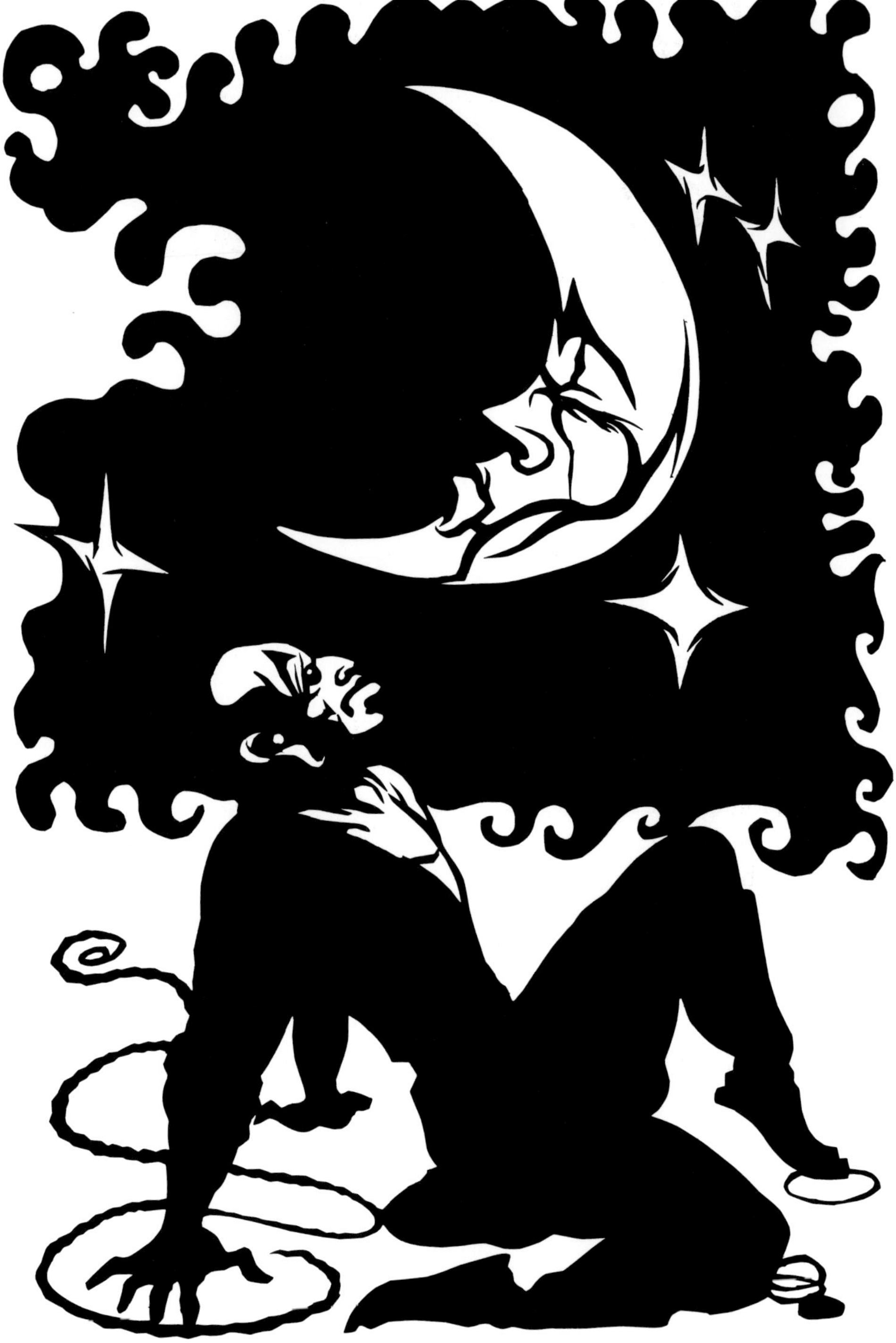

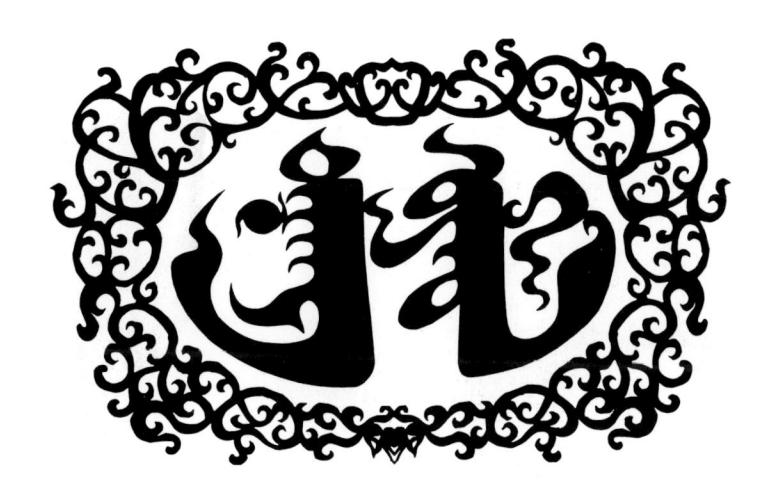

The Fool and the Moon

There was once a man who, in the dark of night, went to fetch water from his well. When he looked down into the deep hole he saw the moon reflected in the water and cried out:

"Oh, no! The moon has fallen into my well!"

The man ran to find a big iron hook, which he tied to the end of a long rope. Slowly he let the hook down into the well, hoping to catch the moon and pull it to safety.

When the hook seemed far enough down in the water, the man began to pull. Suddenly the rope held fast. The man pulled and pulled, not knowing that the hook had become tangled in the weeds at the bottom of the well.

As the man huffed and puffed and pulled and swore, the rope finally broke and the man was flung to the ground onto his back.

Looking up to the sky where the moon now hung, the man smiled as he lay there and said to himself:

"Phew! How heavy it was! Well, no matter. I managed to pull the moon out of the well all by myself and now it is back in the sky where it belongs."

He got up, went home to bed, and dreamed the happy dreams of a hero.

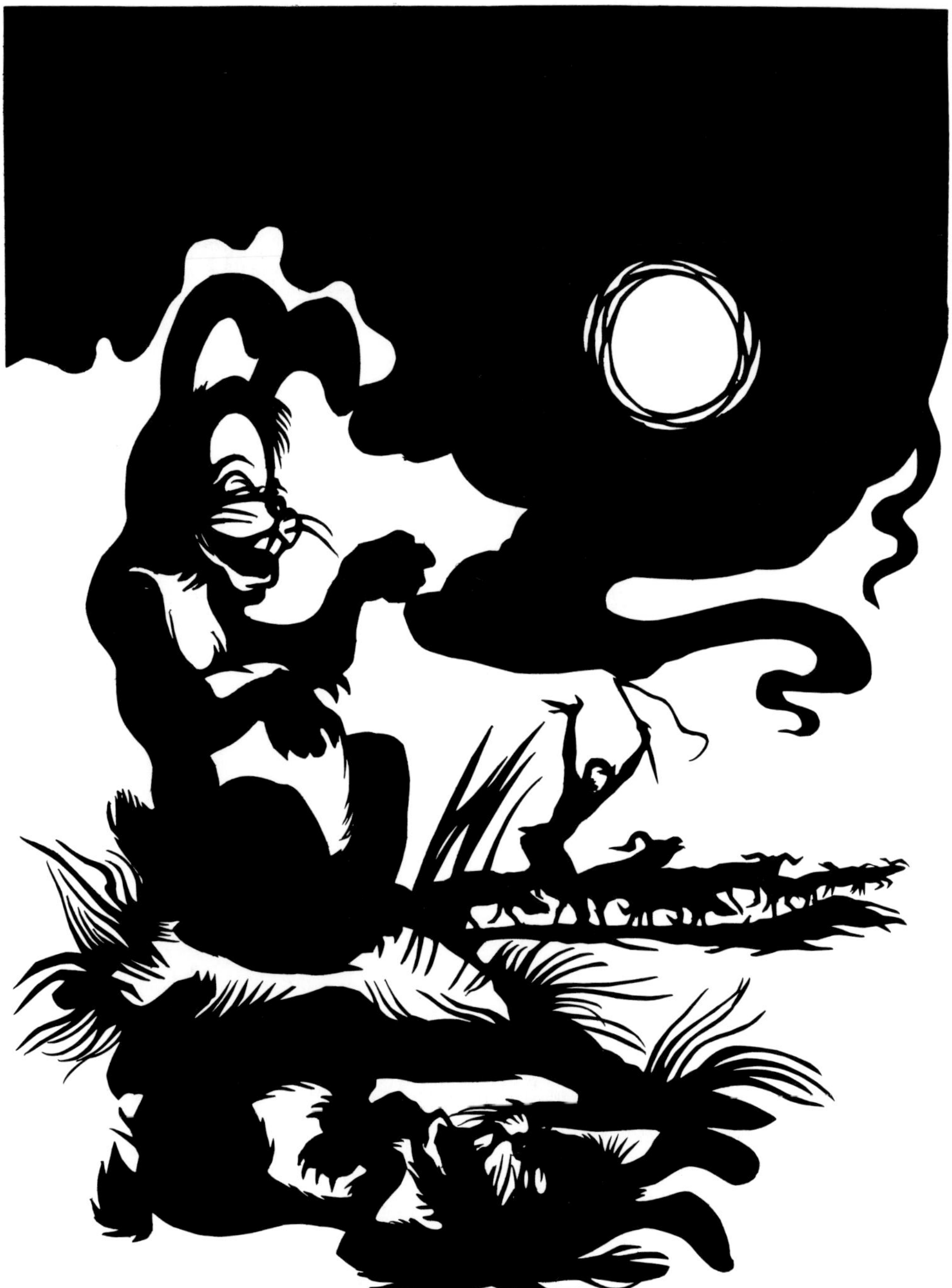

How the Hare Split its Lip

Many, many years ago, the Grand Elder of all the Hares summoned his clan together and said to them gravely:

"Brothers and Sisters. There is not a living thing on this earth that does not know how to defend itself or frighten away its enemy. We Hares are the sole exception: we are afraid of everyone and everything!

"When the leaves on the trees rustle slightly, our hearts sink to our paws; when another creature so much as glances in our direction, we immediately hop away in fright.

"Brothers and Sisters! We are the most wretched of all the animals on the Earth. I have thought this over carefully: it is better that we should all drown ourselves than continue living this way, as the most shameful creatures in the Animal World."

The Hares sighed deeply and flopped their long ears in agreement. Then, with tears of self-pity welling up in their pink eyes, they formed a long line behind the wise Grand Elder, and set out, hopping slowly on their big feet.

Just before reaching the cold waters of their destination, a deep watery pit, a black Magpie swooped out of the skies. Perching on a branch near the long line of weeping Hares, she cried in alarm:

"My dear Hares! What has happened! Where are you all going?"

Without answering the Magpie, the Hares kept on marching to their doom. So the Magpie became insistent:

"Hares! Why are you all so sad? What is the meaning of all these tears? One of you, please tell me what is going on."

One little Hare stepped out of the line and told the Magpie, between loud sniffles:

"Oh, Missus Magpie! No one in this World is afraid of us and we, miserable creatures, are scared of simply everybody. It is best for us to vanish from the face of the Earth."

"What?" cried the Magpie. "What foolishness is this! Stop! All of you."

The whole long line of Hares halted their mournful march and gathered around the commanding Magpie, who told them:

"Hares, you may drown yourselves if you so desire, but before you do, please do as I ask. Please hide behind those bushes over there. A shepherd boy is about to come here to water his sheep. When he arrives, you must all jump out and run in every direction. You'll see for yourselves what will happen. I assure you, Hares are not the only timid creatures on this Earth!"

So saying, the kindhearted Magpie flew away.

The Hares followed the Magpie's instructions and gathered to hide behind the bushes. After a few minutes, a shepherd boy did indeed appear over the hill, herding his flocks towards the spring.

The moment the sheep drew near, the Hares sprang out of the bushes and went bounding and bouncing about. When they finally stopped and looked back, they saw that the sheep had been thoroughly startled and had thundered off in all directions. The poor shepherd boy was desperately trying to stop the wild scramble and was shouting at the top of his voice and cracking his whip.

So surprised were the Hares at what had happened that they stood on their big hind legs and began laughing with glee. They had actually managed to frighten a whole herd of sheep! The Hares laughed so long and so hard that their upper lips split in the middle, and that is why their lips look as they do right up till today.

Need I tell you that the Grand Elder called off his march?

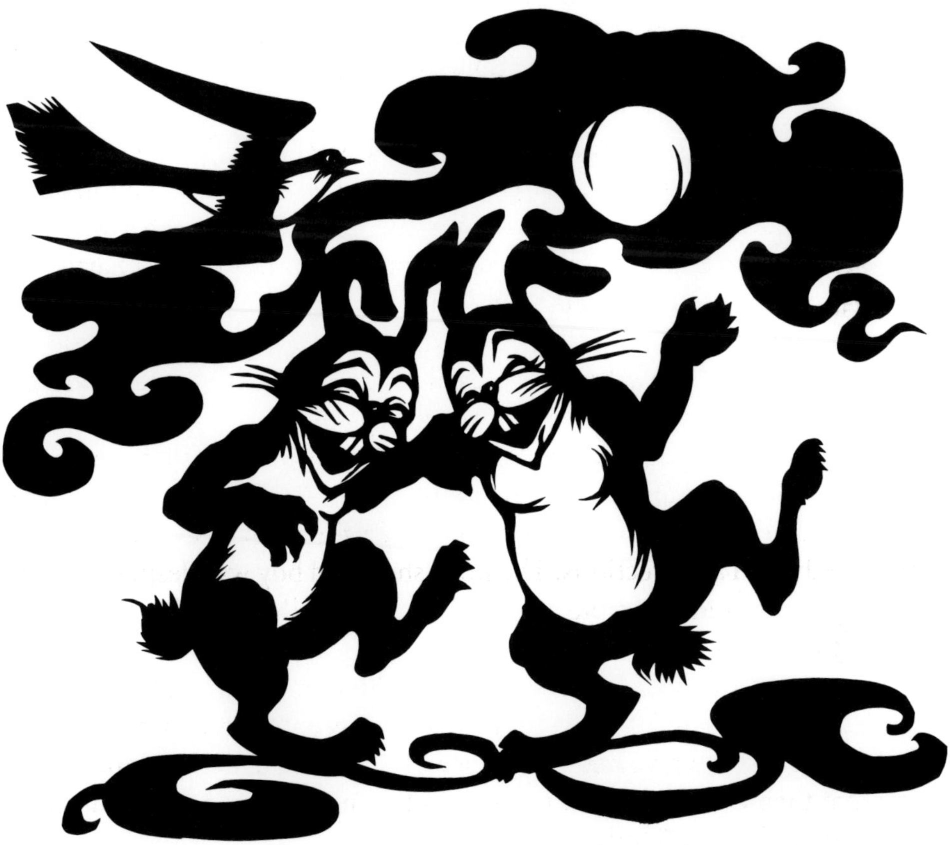

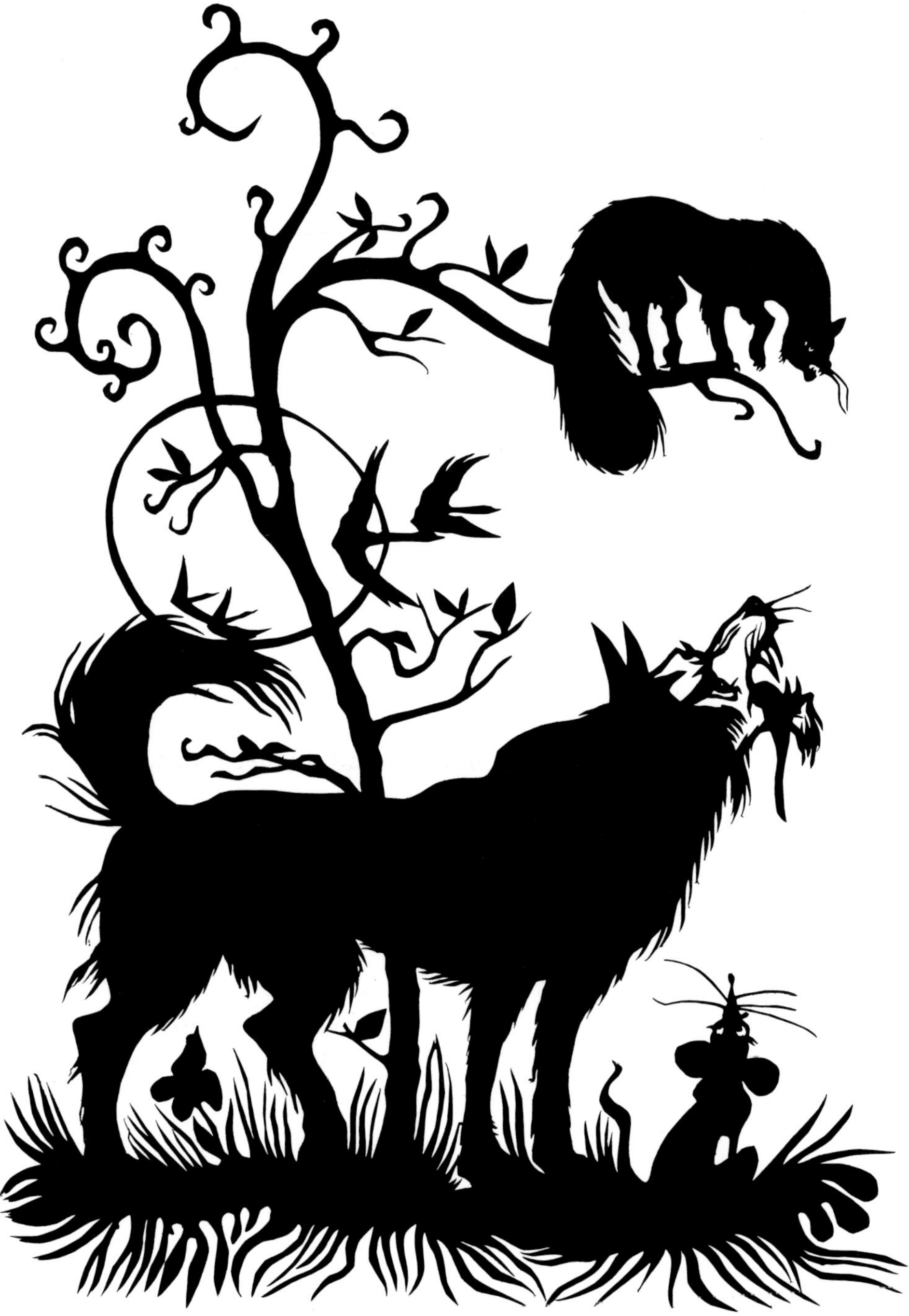

WHY THE DOG, THE CAT AND THE MOUSE HATE EACH OTHER

Once upon a time, a Dog, a Cat, and a Mouse lived peacefully and happily together, the best friends in the world. The Cat and Mouse spent most of the day lazing about and sneaking bits of food, but the Dog worked hard. The big, loyal animal not only looked after his Master's property and his many sheep, horses, goats, and other animals, but also diligently protected his Master's family and *ger* from danger.

The Dog did his job so well, in fact, that one day the Master decided to show the Dog his gratitude. While in town trading sheepskins, the Master had a beautiful certificate made, embossed with shining gold letters. He tied it with a bright red ribbon and that evening presented it to the Dog in a little ceremony, as his family looked on smiling.

The Dog was proud and happy, but the Cat and Mouse, who had witnessed the ceremony from under the bed, became jealous and resentful. When the two animals were alone, the Cat whispered to the Mouse:

"We should take the Dog's certificate with the golden writing, so that the Master will think the Dog does not respect him. Then the Master will like us better! Since you're so small and fast, you steal the certificate tonight and hide it!"

As the sun set and the household slept, the Mouse, on quiet little paws, crept near the sleeping Dog and stole the certificate with the beautiful letters. Instead of just hiding it, however, she gave it to her mouslings, who quickly nibbled it up.

The next morning, the Cat and Mouse came to the Dog and asked: "How did you manage to become the Man's favorite? The King of the Beasts never gave Dogs this privilege!"

The Dog replied: "I know that. But our Master seems to like me very much and he granted me special rights. He even gave me a certificate with beautiful golden letters. Didn't you see it?"

The Cat and the Mouse looked at each other, then, turning to the Dog, said innocently: "What certificate?"

"I'll show you!" Off ran the Dog to find his certificate, so that he could show it to his best friends.

He searched and searched, but couldn't find his certificate anywhere. Near the nest of the Mouse, however, he came across some tiny scraps of shredded paper, some with touches of gold, and he understood what had happened. Hurt and angry, he growled at his 'friends':

"Why, you thieves! You've stolen my certificate and destroyed it!"

And the big Dog charged after the little Mouse, trying to catch her in his big mouth.

Scurrying frantically this way and that, the Mouse squeaked out, pleading with the Dog:

"Brother! It wasn't my idea to steal your certificate! The Cat ordered me to take it!"

So the Dog stopped chasing the Mouse and began bounding after the Cat. The Cat, in turn, began chasing after the Mouse.

"I'm going to catch you and eat you!" the Cat shrieked at the Mouse. "I may have told you to steal the certificate, but I didn't tell you to destroy it!"

The terrified Mouse fled into the safety of her deep hole, while the Cat scrambled up a tree on sharp claws, clinging to a high branch. The furious Dog, betrayed by his best friends, remained below barking.

Since the days of the story of the gold-lettered certificate, the Dog, the Cat, and the Mouse have hated and mistrusted each other.

Every day you can see for yourself that they are still seeking revenge.

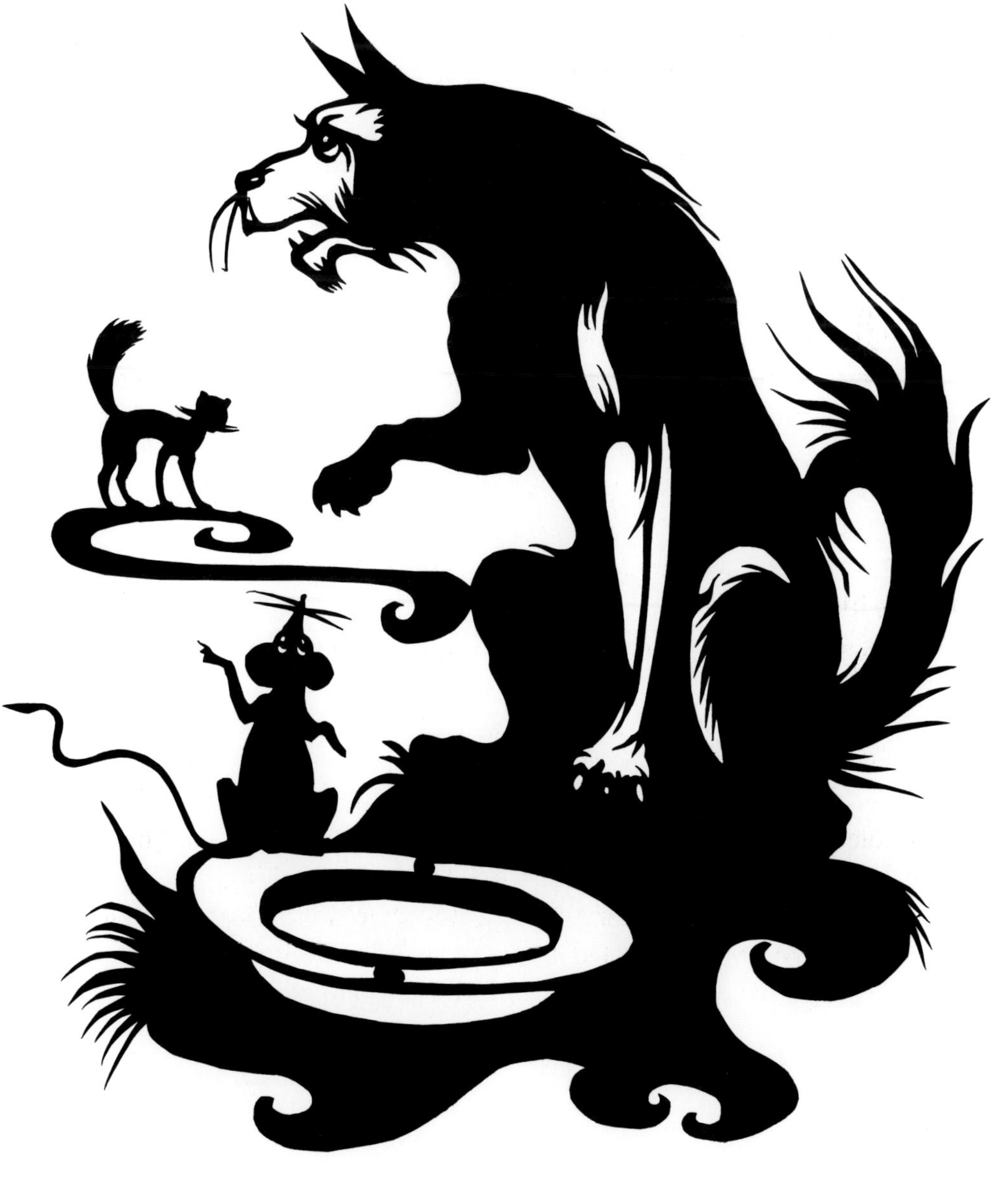

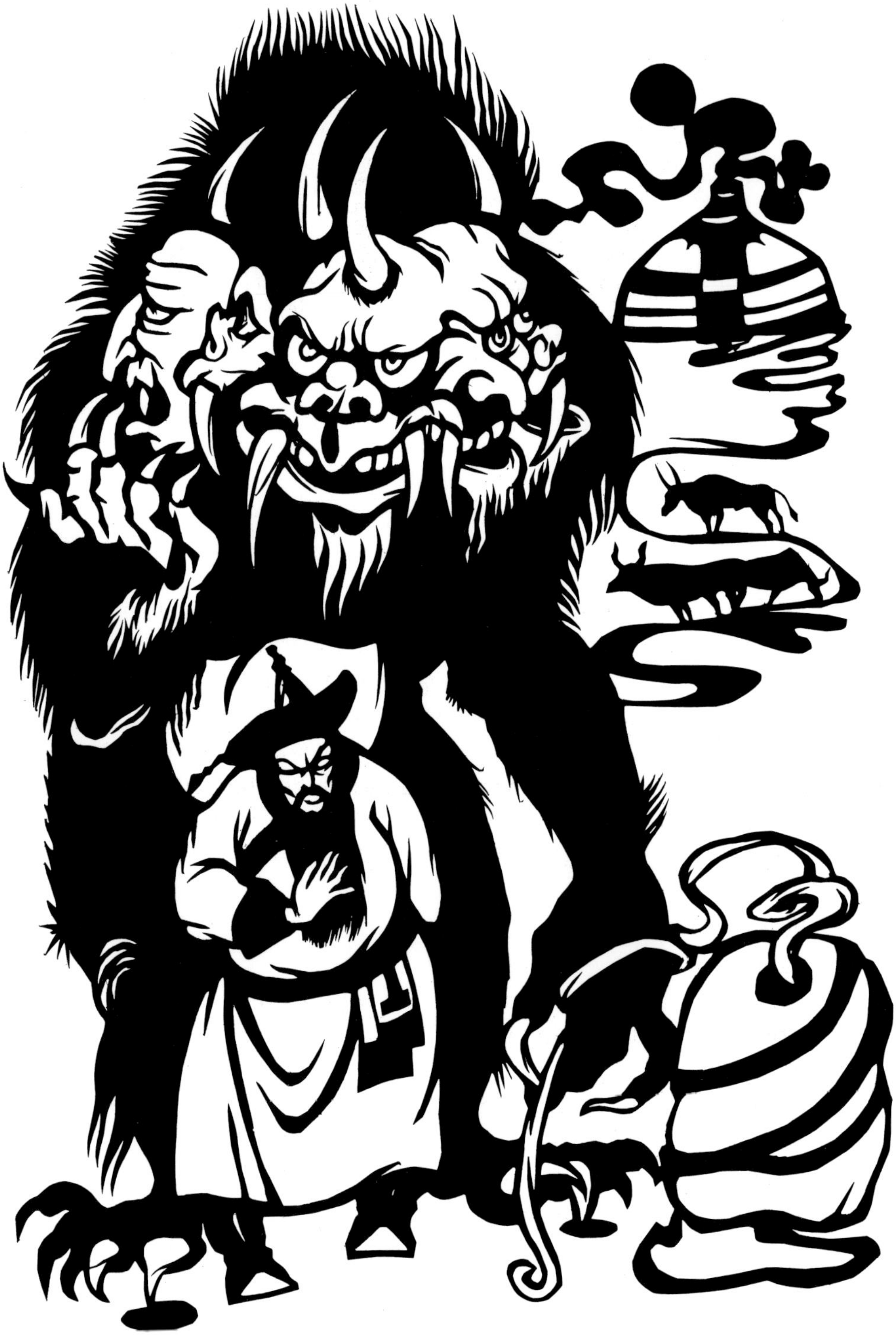

How Mangas the Monster Met His End

On a hot Summer's day on the Mongolian steppe, an old man named Dalantai led his seventy red cows and his one shaggy red bull to the pond for a drink.

As Dalantai's animals lapped up the cool water, the center of the pool began to swirl and foam. Suddenly out of the water there arose a huge and horrible monster with fifteen heads. Seeing such a black and fearsome creature, the animals scattered across the steppe in panic.

It was Mangas the Monster, who had been terrifying the herdsmen, all of them old brothers, for many years, and eating their best animals. Now, at last, the brothers had devised a plan to do away with the monster.

While Dalantai stood glued to the ground, trembling, Mangas opened his fifteen mouths and boomed:

"Old man, I'm hungry! Give me your best animals to eat this instant!"

Dalantai answered:

"Great Mangas, my seventy red cows taste good, that's true, and so does my red bull, but the best thing I have for you to eat are my seventy-layered buttered pancakes!"

"Ummm...pancakes. Get them for me this minute!" roared Mangas.

"I will, oh Great Mangas, but there is one problem. The only way to cut my thick, delicious pancakes is with Tontii's knife."

"You get the pancakes ready," bellowed Mangas. "I'll get Tontii's knife!"

The fifteen-headed monster pulled his immense hairy body out of the pond and lumbered off to Tontii's *ger*.

"Tontii!" cried out Mangas. "Give me your knife right now! I need it to cut Dalantai's pancakes."

"I will give you my knife gladly, Great Mangas," replied Tontii, trembling more than a little before the horrid creature. "But my knife is dull and can only be sharpened with Bintii's grindstone. If you, Powerful Mangas, bring me Bintii's grindstone, we can sharpen my knife together."

Off Mangas trudged, the ground vibrating with his heavy step, to find Tontii's brother, Bintii.

The frightened Bintii, on hearing the black Monster's demand, pointed in the direction of his wheatfield.

"My grindstone, Strong Mangas, is over there. But it's so heavy that it can only be moved to Tontii's *ger* on my brother Hantii's Kazakh carriage!"

"You wait here!" roared Mangas, in hunger and frustration. "I'll get Hantii and his carriage."

He set off again to a distant *ger*. Hantii was there, seated in front of his round home, smoking his silver pipe. Seeing Mangas, he shot up, gasping at the sight of the awful monster.

"Get me your carriage, this instant!" screamed Mangas's fifteen heads, all at once.

"Of course, Great Mangas!" said Hantii. "But my Kazakh carriage is on the other side of the hill, and it can only be moved by Tantii's big white stallion."

"I'll get the stallion! You wait here!" commanded the Monster.

Off he went again, over the hill.

Mangas found Tantii watching his herd of many horses and ordered him to get his big white stallion. Tantii answered:

"Powerful Mangas, my big white stallion is running wild in the hills and I must have Untii's long birch *urga** if I'm to catch him."

More angry than ever, Mangas tromped off to find Untii, who was fishing in the nearby lake. When Mangas demanded to have the *urga*, Untii pointed to the center of the lake and informed all thirty eyes:

"My *urga* is on that island out in the middle of the lake."

"How am I to get across the deep water to that island?" roared Mangas, now extremely hungry and impatient.

Sly Untii informed the terrible monster: "The fastest way is to hang this big magic rock around your neck. It will carry you across the water in no time at all!"

Without thinking, Mangas the Monster heaved up the rock, which had ropes round it prepared by the brothers, and hung it about his thick hairy neck. He plunged into the cold clear lake and quickly drowned.

This was how Mangas the Monster met his end.

Of course, Dalantai, Tontii, Bintii, Hantii, Tantii, and Untii lived peacefully and happily for many more years, laughing every time they thought of Mangas and their magic rock.

Urga: a loop of rope on the end of a long pole, used by Mongolian herdsmen to catch horses.

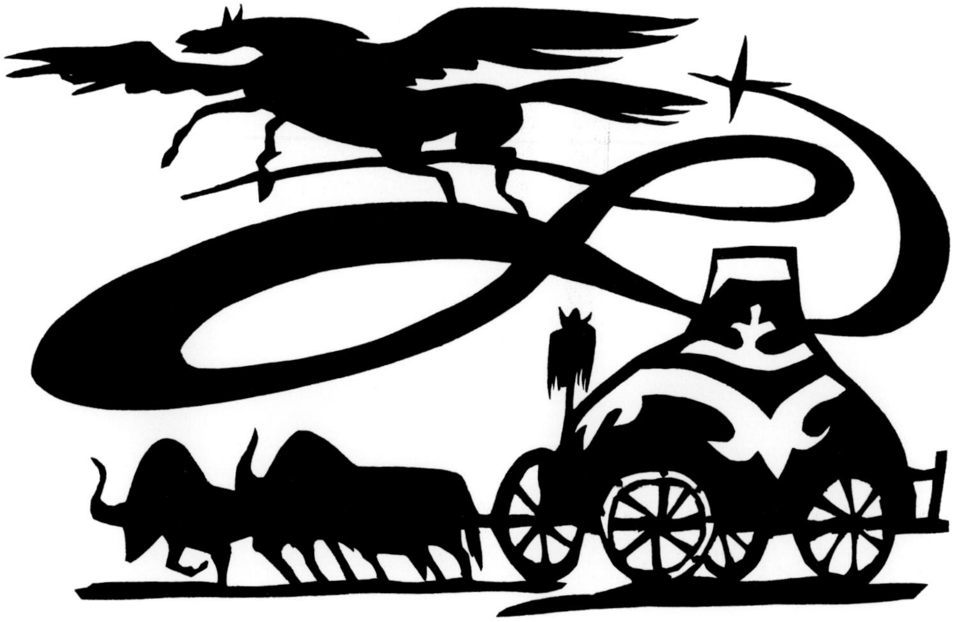

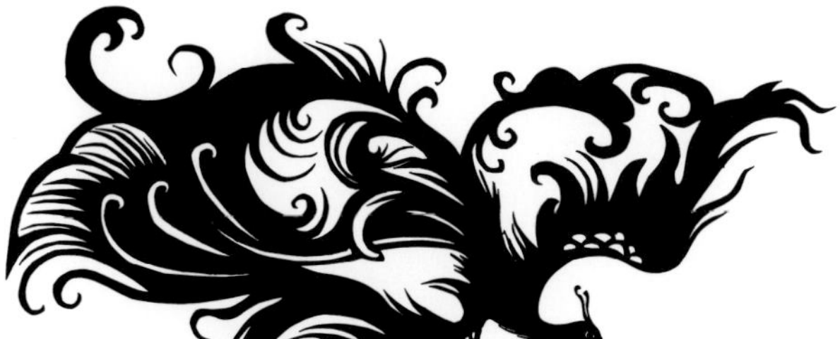